INSIDERS OUTSIDERS

Hidden narratives of care experienced social workers

Edited by
Mary Carter & Siobhan Maclean

Published by
Kirwin Maclean Associates
4 Mesnes Green, Lichfield
Staffordshire
WS14 9AB

enquiries@kirwinmaclean.com
www.kirwinmaclean.com
01543 417800

First published in 2022
Kirwin Maclean Associates
4 Mesnes Green,
Lichfield Staffordshire
WS14 9AB

Graphic design by Tora Kelly
Cover artwork by Saira-Jayne Jones
Inside cover photography by Brett Cummings
Sketches by David Grimm
Printed and bound in Great Britain by 4edge, Essex

ISBN 9781912130528
eBook 9781912130733

This anthology is dedicated to all the care experienced individuals we have lost. A number of the contributing authors have lost loved ones during the publication process. In the UK, people who spent time as children in the care system are 70% more likely to die prematurely than those who did not (Townsend 2020). This has to stop.

Townsend, M. (2020) Childhood in UK care system makes you twice as likely to die earlier, study shows | Life expectancy | The Guardian

In order to empathise with someone's experience you must be willing to believe them as they see it and not how you imagine their experience to be.

- Brené Brown

Each Day, I give you a glimpse of my HEART, sharing my pain... I pray you pay HEED, I want you to SEE me... But we know you NEVER will. Sometimes it SHINES, OTHERS it HIDES, PERHaps one Day... you'll cut THROUGH my SHIELDS.

Contents

Poetry

Essays

About the Authors

That is part of the beauty of all literature. You discover that your longings are universal longings, that you're not lonely and isolated from anyone. You belong.

- F. Scott Fitzgerald

About the Editors

- *Mary Carter*

Mary Carter is a social worker who has lived experienced of the care system.

Mary qualified as a social worker in 2020 at the start of the global pandemic and not long after receiving the prestigious award of student social worker of the year in 2019. Her journey as a newly qualified social worker started in a frontline role within a children in care team. She also sits on fostering and adoption panels for a local authority and independent fostering agencies. In addition, Mary leads skills for fostering training and presents as a guest speaker for various organisations such as secondary schools and independent fostering agencies.

As well as being the founder of the first social work society at her university, Mary was a big part of the transformation strategy for better support for care experienced students.

Mary's personal experience of the care system gives her an invaluable insight into, and understanding of, the painful experiences, rejection and emotional struggles that young people and families face in their lives. Mary brings something different and unique to the profession. Her heart's desire is to support individuals dealing with disadvantage / ill health and to be an agent of change in children's lives. A colleague has described Mary in the following way:

Mary shows remarkable ability to develop effective working relationships with young people and families, her compassion, kindness and commitment to child centred practice is stunning.

As a care experienced social worker, Mary also understands the struggles that those in the care system can face, internally and externally. People are often drawn to social work from their own experiences. As a result of supporting other students, Mary became concerned at the shame and unworthiness those with care experience felt. Mary hopes that this book has a unique way of stopping time and saying: "Let's not forget this". Also, that it shows the value of the lived experienced within the social care profession.

Mary is part of the newly formed Association of Care Experienced Social Care Workers (ACESCW) which aims to assist policy and practice development by providing thought and opinion on best practice. It aims to challenge the stigma and discrimination that can be faced by care experienced social workers through promoting the many positive images and unique insights that are brought to the profession.

Mary would like to dedicate this book to all those that have supported her along her continuing journey of ups and downs, encouraging her to believe in herself and her worth. Also, to all of the young people and families she has been fortunate to support. Mary believes that social work is a gift - you can walk into the lives of wonderful people and make positive changes. For that reason, she will continue to work harder every day.

Mary would like to honour her twin brother for giving her strength and an endless reserve of hope. Even when things don't always work out as planned, he continues to remind her why she went into social work.

Mary would like to give a heartfelt thanks to Siobhan Maclean for giving her the role as co-editor, on such a momentous read. Siobhan has been a fountain of knowledge and emotional hug of warmth to Mary, who is extremely grateful.

Twitter: @marycarter33

- *Siobhan Maclean*

Siobhan Maclean has been a social worker for 32 years and a practice educator for 28 years. Siobhan works independently providing training and consultancy services to social work employers and Universities. She has a particular passion for supporting students and practitioners in the areas of theory and practice and reflective practice. Since the impact of Covid-19 Siobhan has enjoyed working with a group of social work students to develop regular online webinars for social workers. The group that came together to develop these sessions called themselves Social Work Student Connect.

In 1999 Siobhan set up Kirwin Maclean Associates as an independent social work publisher based on the values and ethics of our profession. Siobhan saw many social work textbooks being published by large corporations which didn't necessarily reflect the values and ethics of the profession. She set up Kirwin Maclean (combining her birth name with a married name) in order to develop a publisher which reflected the profession, working towards social work ethics in the development, printing, marketing and distribution of books and resources. She now works with her husband Simon Bates in managing the flourishing publishing business. Siobhan and Simon work to ensure that the publisher gives back to the profession, so the profits generated from the publications go either to charity or to the development of further resources for the profession.

In 2013 Siobhan had a major stroke. This impacted on her work and her understanding of social work in many ways, as experiencing services often does. Since that time, she has not been a direct case holder, although she still supports other social workers in discussing their work directly. She also still works as an off-site practice educator.

Siobhan is committed to ensuring that there is a platform for the voices of people with varied experiences of social work and spends time supporting social workers and people with lived experience to write for publication.

In 2021 along with Wayne Reid, Siobhan edited Outlanders: Hidden narratives from social workers of colour. As she worked on this anthology with Wayne, she realised that a similar book exploring the narratives of care experienced workers would be hugely valuable to the profession and she asked Mary, who she had met through the Social Work Student Connect team, to co-edit the book.

Twitter: @SiobhanMaclean

Website: www.siobhanmaclean.co.uk

PREFACE

On the inside looking out?

- Mary Carter

This book captures the rich voices of social workers who, like me, have care experience. The narratives and messages are a timely reminder to us all that any feelings of shame that we may have felt as a child run deep and continue to be carried as a educated practitioner for many of us.

I hope that people read this with a real personal sense, empathy and understanding. I hope the stories shared here help other care experienced professionals realise they are not alone with the uncomfortable feelings of self-doubt and silent pain they sometimes feel. I hope it also empowers people who have been in care to take ownership of their story and be proud of the champions they are. I feel blessed to be involved with a publication of such inspiration and excellence. I am extremely proud of every author.

Back in 2020, at the start of the Covid pandemic, I had the pleasure of being introduced to the other editor of this book, Siobhan Maclean. I was one of the original members of Student Connect, a team of students collaborating, alongside Siobhan, to prepare and present weekly webinars to student social workers, practitioners and educators around theory and reflection. Our aim was to offer support through the pandemic at a time when learning opportunities became limited and uncertain.

Because of my own work commitments, I had to take a step back from the project, but I continued to join in the weekly webinars in the audience when time allowed. I was particularly encouraged by Siobhan's interest in my journey as a care experienced social worker and the time and effort she took to really understand my views, my passion and my vision.

In March 2021, a year ago, the book Outlanders, compiled and edited by Wayne Reid and Siobhan, was published. A beautiful read. It brought together reflections and experiences of social workers of colour. It left a deep imprint on the social work community. Following its success, and after many interesting discussions, Siobhan and I felt the same voice was needed for care experienced social workers.

When Siobhan asked me if this was a project I wanted to support her in, I didn't hesitate. My answer was an immediate "yes". It sat perfectly with my determination to continue supporting other social workers with care experience.

Despite the pandemic, Siobhan and I finally met face to face to work on the project. A weekend in Northern Ireland, where Siobhan lives, was well spent and very productive. Each day we planned a walk and, with each one, there blossomed so many conversations about the book, our thoughts, our views, our recommendations which absolutely reinforced the value of our working together. It created a real sense of partnership as editors.

Confidentiality was imperative throughout this process. A number of pieces reflect the difficulty social workers can feel about sharing their care status. Allowing practitioners, the space to feel safe, internally and externally was incredibly important to us. I remain immensely aware of the concept of confidentiality in my work with young people and this anthology has made me reflect upon this even more. As a practitioner I will think more about the information I am sharing with other professionals about young people's lives and how this could hinder any trust that has been built.

In this anthology you will read poetry that outlines feelings related to being unheard, unseen and unwanted: that give rise to the isolation and solitude a child in care feels. You will read reflections that describe deep-rooted feelings of shame, labelling, and pain, conveying and evoking powerful waves of emotion. But you will also read narratives that speak of strength, education and identity that will leave you filled with admiration.

Most importantly, the anthology shares personal stories of individuals own past and the vulnerability that comes with practicing as a social worker from facing trauma at a young age. The developed insights, passion and endless reserves of empathy cannot be denied. Something that came to mind from the start of this process, for me, and after a conversation with one of the authors was the potential discomfort and additional emotional wounds that could be created by people sharing their deeply personal stories. Will every author have somebody there to told hold them up if needed? What about for those that are unaware how it could impact them? Will this create a deeper sense of lack of love, a theme that Siobhan and I both felt was missing in the profession for care experienced social workers and generally. Will it interfere with a person's professional and personal self or will it in fact be a spiritual and comforting part of their healing?

I guess, when thinking about my own submission, I didn't really think about how writing down some of my experiences in black and white may impact me. Pulling this apart even more, I know I have developed my own defences against feelings. (Some may refer to this as dissociation) which got me to acknowledge that perhaps I've unconsciously conditioned myself not to feel anything when producing something. Although, how insensitive of me to assume that that would be the same for all authors, a valuable lesson to acknowledge that every individual will have developed their own defences, which may not involve cutting off emotions, therefore the feelings could be even more intense for them. This encouraged me to think about my work with young people and how finding words to help children access their core feelings underneath the surface is so vital. In other words, I need to deepen my own dialogue with them, something I will be more tuned into going forwards in practice. Not every author in this book will be working with children but trauma can be experienced by all ages and adults writing about previous experiences can, for certain, bring back some unresolved trauma that may have been suppressed.

Having read each submission while editing the book, I was blown away. They are all so beautiful in so many ways. These profound stories relay truths in an awe-inspiring manner. The submissions encouraged me to take more ownership of my own story, so I completely shifted my approach. As a result, I felt more comfortable with my own submission.

A friend and former social worker of mine, Elizabeth Tusting, (who has contributed to the anthology) continues to remind me why therapeutic and relationship-based practice will remain at the forefront of all work that I do. I got back in touch with Elizabeth as an adult when feeling particularly alone. She made me feel massively comfortable in approaching her in this way and remains a significant person in my life. I think this input from Elizabeth after leaving care is incredibly important to highlight as it's been pivotal to my own healing and transformation as a practitioner.

To be able to reconnect and have this personal connection with Elizabeth, years after leaving the care system, shines a spotlight on the value of professionals maintaining relationships with young people and the profound impact a social worker can have on a care-leaver's life in years to come. It also demonstrates corporate parenting at its best. It's not within Elizabeth's professional 'role' to invest in me now; she doesn't have to involve me in her life; and she definitely doesn't have a legal duty to care. Yet she chooses to, raising the question about professional boundaries and when it is ok to step outside those constraints and step inside into a personal relationship.

In social work, we learn to expect the unexpected, think on our feet, deal with constant crises in family breakdown, poor mental health, safeguarding concerns and much more. We face harrowing, difficult and upsetting situations. This heart-warming collection of stories also highlights a part of social work that is overlooked and often not thought about enough and while it's tough for all social workers, those who are care experienced may experience these feelings even more intensely. The inner conflict of "not being good enough" feeling "misunderstood" and despite the multiple positive outcomes that these practitioners can help families to achieve, often one mistake or one thing they may do wrong can resurface such negative core beliefs all over again. These same feelings of inadequacy and self-doubt are similarly expressed by social workers of colour in Outlanders.

Many of the pieces relate to strong and painful feelings of shame. Trevor talks about how he was questioned whether he was "ready" for social work after sharing his care status, Hannah mentions how after sharing her experiences with her cohort and peers, she was treated differently and started to question whether she would fit the "ideal image of a social worker". And Marie was laughed at and told that she should look at other careers. I have been left asking myself if there is a high number of care experienced adults that have a real passion and drive to study social work but avoid the stage of applying with the fear of "not being good enough" or failure from internalised narratives that they may have carried through their journey.

It is clear that problems can still be present in contemporary practice too as Victoria J talks about an experience early on into her assessed and supported year of employment where she felt "shut down" and stopped enjoying her work due to a comment made by a previous manager who stated that "if they had known she was care experienced she would not of got the job". Karin Heber asks that readers "see people for who they are" they are not just their care experience alone; they are many other good things too. Celebrate them rather than reduce them to simply a result of their previous experiences.

We know that it is not unusual, for those who have been hurt, to want to move forward by giving back. The influential psychiatrist Carl Jung reflected this in his classic of the "wounded physician" which was described as a person who has struggled, faced adversity particularly in health and has returned to help those that are still hurting (Benziman, Kanni, & Ahmad, 2012).

Social workers who have had their own experience of care know how it feels to have good support from services. They understand what contributes to a comforting, empowering visit with a young person or adult, and what it feels like to be stigmatised by your social worker. Yet, social workers wearing the scars of being in care often feel they have to hide their experiences, because of a fear of being judged by their colleagues and the potential professional consequences.

I hope this book will aid others to understand and learn from the journey that we have taken to pursue a career in social work. Despite the personal and emotional experiences practitioners bring to the role, we all hold one vision in common: to have the greatest impact on people's lives; to help people to see their own strength, and to help them believe in their ability to have a better present and future. Most importantly, we seek to address inequalities through advocacy.

If, by publishing this book, we manage to have a similar impact to that of Outlanders, our decision to go public will have been worthwhile and will, I hope, help our colleagues to understand us a little better.

Being in care doesn't, in itself, define who we are, how we think and how we practice but what it does do is bring with it insight, knowledge and a perspective that those who have not been in the care system could never understand.

I would like to end with a heart felt thanks to you, the reader for dedicating your time and hard-earned money into reading and purchasing this book. And lastly, to all social workers, students, educators, and other social care professionals that continually work to make a difference, thank you for inspiring others to a greater success and thank you for being you.

Benziman, G. Kanni, R. And Ahmad, A. (2012). The wounded healer as a cultural archetype. Comparative literature and culture. 14 (1).

PREFACE

An Outsider looking in?

- Siobhan Maclean

In 2020 / 2021 I worked with Wayne Reid to edit an anthology of narratives from social workers of colour (Outlanders: Hidden Narratives of Social Workers of Colour). Although the idea for the anthology came from me hearing a range of concerning experiences of black students and social workers, I was still shocked and moved by the collection. The whole process of editing that book had a powerful effect on me and I learnt so much about the profession which I have been a part of for 36 years. Working on Outlanders, I realised just how much there is to learn from the narratives of social workers. Having worked with a number of care experienced students I recalled how much I had learnt from the perspective which they were able to bring to situations and I determined to bring together a collection of narratives from care experienced social workers. At the start of the first UK Covid-19 lockdown I had 'met' (online) Mary and was hugely impressed by her energy and passion for our profession and so there was no question who I would approach to work with me on this anthology. Soon after I approached Mary the first meetings took place of what became the Association of Care Experienced Social Care Workers. The timing was perfect, and we decided that we wanted the profits from this book to go towards supporting this vital new, independent, association.

The phrase 'emerging themes' is used a great deal, but of course different themes emerge for different people. We need to explore a range of questions when we are thinking about why certain themes emerge for us in looking at any situation, these include: Who am I? What are my own experiences? Where am I? When am I looking at this situation / collection?

Therefore, to understand why certain themes emerge for me, you the reader, need to know a little about me and my position. I have been a social worker for many years, most recently working predominantly with students, new workers and practice educators. I am passionate about the importance of theory and critically reflective practice for social work. I am not care experienced – I did not grow up in the care system, although I do have some experiences of receiving care services as an adult. As such, I am an 'outsider' and from this position 'looking in' a number of themes emerge for me in this collection of narratives.

Some of the themes I see in this anthology are similar to those that I saw in reading Outlanders. For example, the central importance of trust and how this can be incredibly difficult to build, but very easy to destroy. Of course, there will be some overlap because these are all narratives from social workers and there is always intersectionality and crossover, indeed Rebecca Olayinka has a narrative included in both books. Perhaps the theme which provides the clearest thread between the two anthologies is the importance of love. Love is central to many of the submissions in both books. In fact, the word love appears in this anthology more than a hundred times. A number of authors included in this book refer to the Care Experienced Conference which Ian Dickson founded and chaired. One of the results of this conference was 10 top messages which I try to convey in all of my work – the number one message is *"we need more love in the care system, including displays of positive physical affection."* As social workers we need to explore with urgency how we can bring this about. The powerful anonymous poem on page 188 tells us that 'you accept the love you think you deserve' the question remains, how do we ensure that care experienced people know that they deserve all the love in the world? In Outlanders, Narinder Sidhu tells us *"Love is always the way, just ask those who have felt it."* In this anthology I was struck by how many social workers have not felt it. This has left me pondering the question, what can we do to ensure that the people we work with really *feel* loved?

In the notes that I developed as the submissions came in, I wrote that I suspected the most commonly repeated word in the anthology would be shame. So many of the reflections refer to shame, I was particularly struck that Richard Devine, who is the son of a care experienced social worker (we specifically approached Richard to contribute) talks a great deal of shame, demonstrating the inter-generational issues that social work is learning so much about. David Anderson says very powerfully *"poverty was, and is, a political choice, is something that should shame all those responsible."* This helps us to recognise that it is the profession, and those of us within it who allow the oppression of care experienced social workers to continue, that should be shamed. Marie's powerful title *"Shaking of the shame"* made me think about a quote from Elizabeth Lowell, "Some of us aren't meant to belong. Some of us have to turn the world upside down and shake the hell out of it until we make our own place in it." We need to shake the profession and make a place for care experienced workers at the very centre of it. However, when it came together it was clear that the most repeated word in the anthology is love. Maybe it is having more love in the care system that will shake the profession?

Love means many things, but to me perhaps the central component of love is that it brings with it a sense of belonging. In fact, Brené Brown connects the two very clearly when she says, *"those who have a strong sense of love and belonging have the courage to be imperfect"*. Mary has talked to me many times about her drive for perfection and she sees this as a shared experience with care experienced people. When I reflected on the connection between love and belonging, I think I developed a deeper understanding of Mary's perspective. Almost every narrative shared in this anthology contains something about seeking a sense of belonging. Marie tells us that she feels that she doesn't belong anywhere and when I thought about this, I understood the title of the anthology in a new and different way. If the authors in this anthology don't have a sense of belonging to the profession, then where can they feel they belong?

The book also contains many messages about conflict. Laura Bye tells us that her own feelings have been conflicted; in 'You don't know what it feels like' the anonymous writer tells us that she knows what conflict feels like on many levels; Victoria-Maria shares her identity conflict with us, and Dr Trevor Rodgers-Gray cites Newcomb et al. (2017) who identify the potentially conflicting internal roles that may be experienced by care experienced people. Indeed, what has struck me the most about all of this conflict is that most of it is inner conflict. David Grimm's work especially shows how 'enemies' emerge where there is conflict and I wonder whether some of the authors need a critical friend but feel they are surrounded by critical enemies. As I was reading the submissions I wrote in my own reflective journal "...*it must be exhausting dealing with all of this conflict, and when it is inner conflict what is that doing to the individual's sense of self?*" Ian Thomas reminds us that love is always the antidote to conflict, focusing us again on the central importance of love in social work.

A dear friend and care experienced colleague of mine, Paul Yusuf McCormack talked often about the need to "put love into social work." The weekend that Mary and I worked on the final editing of the collection was the anniversary of Paul's death. Of course, that had an impact on the way that I saw the submissions, but one particular thing that jumped out at me was the use of the phrase 'broken smile.' Two of the poems included in the book use this phrase which was the title of one of Paul's poems and paintings. Paul called for us all to BE the difference and I hope that readers of this anthology may think about how they can really be the difference. For this reason, I have (with the consent of Paul's family) ended this anthology with one of Paul's poems which calls for us to Be the difference. Paul wasn't a social worker, but he was a foster carer, and he trained many social workers. I know that Paul would have been immensely proud of the authors in this book.

Throughout the Covid19 pandemic I have been working on the need for more kindness within the profession. I wonder whether, as we have progressed with the professionalisation of social work, we have moved away from some of the basic fundamental virtues on which it should be based. I have started to explore what our knowledge base says about kindness, and it is really hard to find the word anywhere. It doesn't appear in UK social work professional standards and it's not there in the theory base. I have literally been hunting for the word. Everything I look at now I am looking for the word kind. You will find kindness here. I found it. The word appears in the narratives in this anthology 18 times. This is what 'insider' experience provides. What matters is sometimes difficult to measure and, unfortunately, we have allowed the focus in social work to move towards what is easy to measure. Love and kindness matter. They may be difficult to quantify and to process in data, but this anthology shows how kindness impacts and how it can be, in fact, a life and death matter.

I have always been very conscious about the use of language as a social worker and recognise that language and meaning need to be kept under constant reflection. I have learnt something new about the use of language in my role in working on this anthology. We have long known that the word 'placement' is inappropriate when we are talking to children and young people about where they live and where they call home (which may or may not be the same place). I haven't used the word placement in my social work practice for many years, and yet I use the word placement in relation to the work that I do with students and practice educators every day. Reading this anthology has made me reflect on how this might feel for care experienced social work students and so in the future I will ask students about their choice of word for their practice learning environment.

When Mary and I read the submissions, we provided some feedback and thoughts for the authors. We did not change the submissions, because they belong to the contributors.

We wanted to take real care of what we were sent. These narratives are precious and should be treated as such. I have had a great deal of feedback that Outlanders is a 'beautiful book' – which I am proud of. Books containing narratives like these should have time spent on them. What they look like and feel like matters. Therefore, Mary and I had lots of conversations about the design of this book. The cover was inspired by a painting submitted by Saira Jayne at the start of the process. We were also sent a number of photos by Victoria-Maria, and we asked if we could include these within the book – they give a powerful sense of the experiences that children and young people have in the care system. Other photographs in the anthology come from student social workers showing their experiences during the Covid-19 pandemic which will undoubtedly impact on social work for many years to come. These are not 'beautiful' images, but they are authentic and there is beauty in this.

Something that has surprised me during the process of curating this anthology is that there is a lack of awareness (on many levels) of what it means to be care experienced within the profession. When we first advertised the book and put out a call for care experienced social workers, I was contacted by a number of people wanting to contribute. They had a great deal of work experience, but they were not care experienced. I was surprised by the lack of awareness around the term care experienced within the profession, although I reflected that perhaps we should have been clearer about what we meant in the original call. Even after an explanation of the term, one person was quite persistent in their emails to me which became more insistent that their professional experience should be equally valued, they seemed to be cross that I was (in their words) 'excluding' them. In her reflection, Kyla asks why professional experience of the system is valued whilst personal experience of that same system is simultaneously devalued. This is an excellent question and one which requires every reader to reflect on the way that they view the experiences of their colleagues.

As we are finalising this anthology and preparing to go to print, I have been working on presentations for World Social Work Day 2022. The theme this year is ´Co-building a New Eco-Social World: Leaving No One Behind´. In reading the submissions we received I have sadly become even more aware that we are, in fact, leaving people behind within our own profession. The United Nations offers a really helpful framework for analysing who is left behind which contains five areas to consider – discrimination; geography; vulnerability to shocks; governance (which includes law, policy, institutions, voice and participation) and socio-economic status. As social workers we could use this framework in a range of ways to help us to consider who is being left behind and how it is happening. Reflecting on this framework I can see many concerns in relation to care experienced social workers, especially in contemporary social work which has been changed so much by recent events. Social workers are working from 'home' what does this look like for care experienced workers and how is it impacting on that sense of belonging that has been identified as vital in this collection?

Prospera Tedam was a contributor to Outlanders, she has developed the excellent 4D2P model for anti-oppressive practice in social work (Tedam 2021) this calls for us to have open and honest **d**iscussions where we are likely to **d**iscover peoples' experiences of oppression. We have a responsibility to reach **d**ecisions about the mechanisms and structures of oppression and what we can do to **d**isrupt these. The 4Ds need to be underpinned by the 2Ps – an understanding of our own **p**ower and **p**rivilege. When you are reading this anthology, I urge you to use the 4 Ds and 2Ps. Think about your own power and privilege, see the narratives as the start of a discussion with colleagues where you can discover what is happening for care experienced social workers and please make some decisions about what you can do to disrupt the oppression faced by your colleagues. The Cambridge Dictionary defines the word disrupt as "*to prevent something, especially a system, process, or event, from continuing as usual or as expected*". We must disrupt what is happening for care experienced social workers within the profession. Some of the reflections offer the reader specific advice for their practice, others help us to explore for ourselves what we may be able to do to really bring about change. Victoria J tells us that she has healthier roots in the profession thanks to the professionals and organisations who have been *"inclusive to all, to give colleagues room to grow"*. Victoria also shares with us photographs of her sculpture of uplifting hands. Ask yourself, what is in your hands? What can you do to change the experiences of care experienced social workers within the profession? Then do it and BE the difference.

Tedam, P. (2021) Anti-Oppressive Social Work Practice. (London) Sage, Learning Matters.

Why Insiders Outsiders?

When we spent a weekend together working on the anthology Mary and I discussed the title which developed into Insiders Outsiders. I wanted to a title which had some synergy with the original Outlanders title conceived by Wayne, but of course it needed to capture the connections within the narratives in this anthology. I started off with the thought that the authors in this book have 'inside' knowledge about the care system that they are now working within, so I wondered about simply 'Insiders.' However, as we worked through the submissions and went on walks together to discuss our thoughts, we reflected together that although the authors were insiders they were often being treated as outsiders. Once we thought about this, we began to see words that started with IN or OUT in the submissions and as we pulled these together it was really thought provoking.

More than 80 words started with in, including:

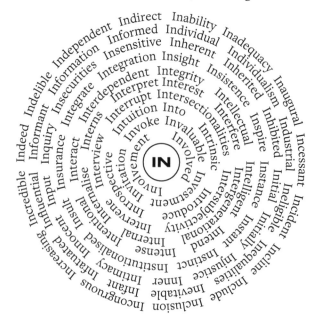

Pulling out these words and thinking about how they might play out in social work practice provided Mary and I with some really interesting reflections. There were a few words that we added, such as innermost; inseparable; invasive; intense; indicative and indefensible. On later reflection when I was revisiting the international definition of social work:

> *"Social work is a practice-based profession and an academic discipline that promotes social change and development, social cohesion, and the empowerment and liberation of people. Principles of social justice, human rights, collective responsibility and respect for diversities are central to social work. Underpinned by theories of social work, social sciences, humanities and indigenous knowledges, social work engages people and structures to address life challenges and enhance wellbeing."*
>
> (IFSW and IAASW 2014)

I had the realisation that this book is all about 'indigenous knowledge' the authors included in this anthology have a unique insight and we must learn from this knowledge. Historically (and still) indigenous communities are oppressed. Also referred to as first nations and first people, this must help us to recognise that the people that social work seeks to support must come first. As we start to more widely recognise the need to decolonise the curriculum in social work this must apply to the inclusion of the knowledge that care experienced people bring.

There are fewer words in the narratives that begin with 'out' – just 7:

Again, Mary and I added quite a few including outcast; outpouring; outranked; outspoken; outmanoeuvred; outdated; outnumbered; outperforming and outpaced. But it was perhaps in thinking about phrases beginning with 'out' that Mary and I really started to reflect. Are care experienced adults out of sight and out of mind in the profession? Are some professions considered to be out of bounds for care experienced adults? And does this anthology help us to be out with the truth?

Outlanders was the first book that Siobhan produced which had an inside as well as outside cover. Of course, we wanted to continue this style into this anthology but since a central theme of the anthology is the idea of inside and outside, we thought about the way that the cover could perhaps demonstrate some of what came through in the book around this theme. The outside cover artwork is by Saira-Jayne Jones and the cover was built around her initial artwork submission. Paintings are an impression of what something is like. As an outsider that is all we have – an impression. Insiders have the real-life experience. We therefore wanted the inside of the cover to be 'real'. Brett Cummings, a social work student, was kind enough to support us with some photographs that might represent some of the words that we felt came through in the initial submissions. This cover therefore represents that way that inside knowledge is real, while outside experiences give us an impression.

We hope that the title of this publication will prompt you and your colleagues to have some reflective conversations. We need a revolution of love and kindness in the social work profession. Are you in or are you out?

IFSW and IAASW (2014) International definition of Social Work. Available online at Global Definition of Social Work – International Federation of Social Workers (ifsw.org)

We don't care about whose DNA has recombined with whose. When everything goes to hell, the people who stand by you without flinching - they are your family. Family is about who is willing to hold your hand when you need it the most.

- Jim Butcher

REFLECTIONS

Why I want to become a social worker

- Carolina Caires

I want to study a social work degree in university and become a social worker because I would love to empower, motivate and support children that have unfortunately had to face traumatic life experiences at such young age. I want to bring positivity into their lives, make them believe in themselves and be confident about their goals. As a young person that is familiar to the care system, I want to make sure that children who experience care don't allow such labels to define them and continue to pursue their dreams like everyone else.

I have been doing work with the Participation and Engagement officer for children services in my local authority for about 2 years, this has bought opportunities for young people such as fun activities, parties, awards events and even virtual events. Within this opportunity I was very fortunate to have been involved in interviewing many job roles for panels but mostly social workers, this was started during the COVID lockdown. Interviewing social workers, made me realise what type of social worker our young people deserve. For me, the social worker our young people deserve is a social worker who is ready to listen, communicate, connect and understand them. Someone who is dedicated to the job with passion for helping children and lead them in the right direction, a person who wants to represent their young person in their best interest.

Apart from this I have been doing work experience within the children services sector at the Council and attended trainings for social workers. This has expanded my knowledge when it came to working with young people, I learnt that it is not just a social worker who handles the case alone there are many different people with different job roles that have a part in the case in order for it to be successful.

My personal experience both in and out of care has made me passionate about helping children, empower them and make sure their voices are heard, because they are important, they need to be seen and heard. Hopefully, as a future social worker I want to bring more opportunities for our young people in my local area. I want to believe that in the near future our young people feel safe to speak up and use their stories to inspire others. Lastly, I want to make sure that they are seen as children with dreams and goals not labels and case numbers.

Same, Same, but different!

- David Anderson

I was brought up in a housing scheme in the 70s and 80s, it was a poor area. I mention this to remind that poverty - in all its guises and so relevant today - is most probably *the* major factor in many young people being brought into a care situation. That poverty was, and is, a political choice, is something that should shame all those responsible.

In my family home, there existed, financial difficulty, alcohol abuse, criminal activity, parental conflict, physical and emotional abuse, mental health issues, and love. Let's never forget the love. Because it usually exists, even in homes where the situation is not appropriate for a child to live. It is important to remember if a child is then moved into a 'care' situation where love is missing, then they may lose one of the most important things in life. The feeling of being loved.

From an early age, I was 'in trouble' at school. Back then, some teachers belted instead of supported you. I began to run away from home from the age of 8. My father wasn't good for me and the arguments at home were too much sometimes. Aged 10, I was given a social worker. No family support was put in place. Therefore, the situation didn't change. I was then taken into (so-called) care. I was placed in a semi-secure environment with around 60 other vulnerable young people. We wore the same clothes, lived in 'units' and doors were locked. I was offered drugs on my first night. I took them because I wanted to fit in with the peer group; a collection of children with a range of support needs, all of whom had lived in situations that inhibited their development in some way. It was a wild, dangerous, and often - for all the wrong reasons - exciting place to be. The setup was just like a prison, and it served only to exacerbate the problems in my life.

What followed, was an all-too-familiar tale of placement moves, abuse of various kinds, and a real lack of love. All through this 6-year period, the narrative was that I was a bad kid. From my old Granny - who loved me dearly - who could never understand why I was in a *bad-boys home*, neighbours who didn't want me playing with their children, teachers who told me I would amount to nothing, police who treated me like I wasn't entitled to the same rights as others, social workers who threatened me with secure care on a continual basis (to the point I actually wanted to go) and a myriad of care-workers who talked at me or about me as if I was something to be done about. Little wonder I rejected adults at every turn and rejected *their* society. I wasn't a part of that society. I was something other, the underclass, a care-kid. I just had to survive any way I could or die. I don't exaggerate when I say that. I could make too long a list of those who are now dead from that time. I know others who have experience of losing people they know from the care system far too early, dead because of a lack of true care. Indeed, there have been very recent headlines which show that this is still happening today. It is heart-breaking that this is the case.

At 16, I was dumped - ill-prepared - in my own flat. I was seen once a fortnight for an hour by a busy worker. I lost my flat soon after, in truly disturbing circumstances. I was beaten out of my own home and worse. I slept on the stairs in a multi-storey block of flats after I was found sleeping in my friend's assisted accommodation. The care-workers there put me out into the cold in September to sleep rough. The narrative, and actions towards us, was such that this was accepted as normal. The workers accepted that I would be homeless because *that's just what happens to care-kids.* You know what? I accepted it too. After all that had happened to me, it was normal for me to be there, freezing, on cold, piss-stained stairs, in a multi-storey block of flats. It was all too normal for the society I was rejecting, a society that had rejected me, a society that accepted this treatment of children. The story could and should have been so much different. Again, the fact that it is not and that today there are similar stories occurring should bring shame on those who could change it in an instant.

Over the next four years, like too many others from my time in care, I had problems with drugs, alcohol, violence and gambling. No-one batted an eyelid. The youth justice system cranked into action (another system short on common sense). I was imprisoned several times. At no point was I offered support. If I had died, no-one would have been surprised. However, I was lucky to meet some people who truly cared. They helped shape me, seen past the labels, the pervasive narrative, those commonly held ideas about *people like me*. And, when I was ready, I began to turn my life around. Now, what is important to say here is this. I received some genuine love during my time in care, some of those who supported me have left an indelible mark on my very being. I live by their moral code, I act as they acted with me, I try to emulate them every day. Why? Because they showed me genuine care, love through deeds and words. Davie, who taught me about right and wrong, Mike, who taught me about injustice and therefore justice, and Irene, who taught me about human warmth and kindness. Oh, and another very important thing I mention again. *All* those I was in care with were more than the narrative pitted against them. They were all capable of being a real success.

So, the next part of my story goes like this. I returned to my mother's, aged 20, after another short stint in prison. I asked her to take me in, to my eternal gratitude, she did. Things had changed at home. My Dad was long gone, and my Mum was in a much better place than before, managing her depression to the extent she was a success in both her personal and professional lives (not that they are truly separate entities). I started college, an access to university course for those with no formal qualifications. I passed and went on to Uni. That access course was a real turning point. Education is truly a route towards a positive future. However, there must be other supports in place, it can be a real challenge to manage full-time education alongside all the other demands of being an adult citizen.

At University, I continued to make progress, my mind was now open to all that a good education can offer, not least some understanding of what it means to be a citizen and the rights and opportunities that I could enjoy if I participated in society. I no longer completely believed the narrative I had been subject to. After two years of study, I began working in a local homeless shelter. I especially related to the young people who entered the establishment. I pushed a positive narrative to and about them. At times, it was rewarding. Too often, I was disgusted at the way young people in their situation were written off. After a while, a chance meeting delivered an opportunity to move job.

I was encouraged to apply to work with a new charity working with children and young people deemed *hardest to reach*. Personally, I've never found any young person hard to reach. Sometimes, I've had to go to where they were, at the time they were available, and with a language that they spoke, but never were they *unreachable*. I remember well that I, at my most self-destructive, still spoke to people who were genuinely interested. To get this job, I had to have a special meeting with the board of directors, to discuss my convictions and recount some of my life story. Following a long discussion, they decided to give me the go-ahead to work for the charity. They saw the potential and weighed it up against the perceived risk.

Then, I had to have another meeting. This time, with the head of Children Services in the Local Authority. Again, I spoke about my life and circumstances. The head of services gave the charity the go-ahead to employ me. This meant I would work indirectly for the Local Authority. This was my chance, the process of re-confession, revisiting the past, and disclosing extremely personal information, had paid off. It hadn't been a pleasant experience, but I had some faith in those who were encouraging me. They were pushing a positive narrative about young people in care. They understood the difficulties faced before, during, and after care.

The job was a real opportunity, and I enjoyed the work. I was offered a full-time position after a three-month probationary period. Within two years, I was promoted on two occasions. I wanted to develop my practice further and decided to apply for the new professional social work master and was successful at the interview. I went through the same process of revisiting my history with the University human relations officer or, to put it another way, a complete stranger. It seemed like it was a case of 'going through the motions', as if they were ticking a box.

For my first placement, I *again* had to apply for a disclosure form. *Again*, I had to sit down with senior management and go through my history and personal circumstances. The director - an experienced woman with some 40 years of practice under her belt - had no hesitation in saying yes. As far as she was concerned, I was as any other student. She told me, *I don't need to know this stuff, it isn't relevant now, we shouldn't even be having this conversation.* That was the narrative I needed to hear. It made going through all my history feel worth it, even if I felt it wasn't really necessary after all I had achieved. The placement was successful. I was even asked back, so I could continue with some of the support. I agreed, because I value continuity of support (I'd watched enough care workers come and go in my own life). I understood relationships were key and even though it meant a long train journey each day, I wanted to do what I believed in.

I was happy (if not tired) and felt good about myself and my efforts. The narrative was continuing to change in my head. Maybe, I wasn't so bad after all. I passed all the relevant modules at university. All the while, I continued to support young people for the charity, continued to work for the same Local Authority. I now believed that I had shown my suitability for the type of work I was training for and that my care story would no longer be an issue. I thought the negative narrative of my care experience had been replaced by the positive narrative of my proven track record within the social care sector.

The third and final placement meant taking up a formal statutory role in a social work department. *Again*, I had a meeting with a senior human resource manager to explain my history and speak of my current circumstances. The feedback was positive, and I believed I would start the following week. This was not to be the case. Two days later I received a call informing that I was to be rejected. The head of social work, the Director, had been informed of the situation and decided they *could not take the risk of giving me a placement*. Not only was this the self-same Local Authority that I had been working for during the last three or so years (and showing how ridiculous his position was, I would continue to do so), it was also where I had experienced five years of often abusive care. It was the same Local Authority who were responsible for shunting me around numerous placements then turfing me out, ill-prepared and alone at 16. What this says about their idea of what social work is actually for is a question I have pondered on more than one occasion.

I felt discriminated against. Why now? Why after all the success and hard work was my suitability being questioned? Why was I being denied opportunity? Would it be like this forever? Would I ever get a job in social work? My treatment seemed at odds with what I was being taught. I was of a mind to quit. The old habit of thinking that I would never be a part of *their* society returned, that their narrative of me as a *risk* would always be the dominant one. However, some discussion with trusted individuals soon allowed me to let the dark cloud pass and to continue with my own personal development goals.

The thing is the contextual history to my situation explains why I ended up going through what I went through. None of which the Director cared to ask me about. He didn't want any relationship with me. The news was delivered cold by someone under his management. However, I wanted to speak to him and called his office. I asked him why. He simply told me that *he* couldn't take the risk. In this situation, I wasn't a person to be valued for my history, my progress, my potential future. I was to be considered nothing more than a potential risk. Given I had worked indirectly for the Local Authority for over three years, it could only mean I was a risk to him personally. *In what way*, I thought? To his career? It can only be that. What else could it be? Or did he consider me a risk to others? To children and young people? Was I a risk to children, young people, and my colleagues or him personally, or both? Either way, it was a real blow, one which I felt in the pit of my stomach.

Before the end of that very short conversation, I said to him,

"don't you think a Local Authority that did not provide me with appropriate care, that moved me from pillar to post, left me in abusive situations, did none of those things you now publicly call for as being necessary (he was a very vocal director). Do you not think that maybe you should take that qualified risk, given that others have given me their professional seal of approval and my career is developing well? Am I not deserving of that chance?"

His simple reply.

I cannot take that risk.

I hung up the phone and considered the devastation he had just wrought upon my life. I am sure he continued with the business of the day. Not for him a discussion to see if he could use his so-called expertise and experience to make a more informed judgement call. Just a straightforward rejection based on his own notion of risk as it related to what it meant to his position. The fact the buck stopped with him was enough to dismiss the mounting evidence that I was an asset to the profession. Just think of how many other people have had that rug pulled from under their feet or who have never even bothered trying because they knew the odds were stacked against them. Indeed, many young people who have experienced care are written off way before they get as far as I did. The fact I made it as far was basically an anomaly. Wrongly so. All of those I walked through life with during my five years in care had the potential to be a success. They were denied by a system designed to work against their potential. I repeat, the fact it is still happening today should bring shame upon those who could change it in an instant. For those who do succeed in surmounting the barriers, they are faced with a profession that often continues the stigmatisation and discrimination they have already experienced. The social work profession too needs to look at the stigma attached to care experienced social workers. I have heard too many stories of individuals feeling it necessary to hide their history because of a pervasive notion that somehow it is something negative or not necessary to mention.

Fortunately, because of two supportive social workers who took it upon themselves to act, another Director of Social Work took the opposite approach. He invited me for a meeting to discuss the placement and gave me his decision direct to my face. I completed a successful placement and was recommended by the team leader to be given a post within the team. You would think that the discrimination would've stopped there. Nope. I went for the post on the recommendation of my supervising senior only for the human relations manager in that Local Authority to deny me because the risk was his to take (he was apparently miffed that the two social workers had circumvented his position to make a direct approach to the director and was demonstrating his authority). Obviously, making it the responsibility of one individual to arbitrarily decide on the basis of a perceived risk to themselves is wrong. Careers should not hang in the balance thus, on the whim of one person. A change is needed, a new process based upon support and clarity would help to change the discrimination too many are faced with.

Soon after, I did get a job. Another supportive social work manager decided to give me a role (there are many out there). It seemed easy enough for her when presented with the facts. The post went well. Since then, I have completed a master's in social research, focussing on the education of care-experienced people. I now - amongst other things - teach social work students and run a therapeutic farm alongside my wife. I also campaign and play a part in agitating for the necessary changes that will see children understood, valued, and given opportunity to thrive. Because every child deserves to enjoy a life free from unnecessary stigma and discrimination.

At my 'worst' (when I was let down the most). I was written off by almost everybody. In considering all I have achieved – despite the lack of support (from some quarters) from the very profession set up to assist people to do overcome adversity in their lives - is there anyone who could say that I wasn't worth the *risk*. However, that isn't even the point. The real point of social work is to provide the right support at the right time without any contingent factor. It should be provided because it is the right thing to do not because of any imposed *outcome*.

Social work should face up to the very real stigma attached to being care experienced. There should also be a process set up whereby those who were criminalised during their stay in care are given support to have those convictions considered in the context of their lives at that time. We know that people who experienced care are many times more likely to have convictions, we should therefore consider them as a *result* of that care. Printed information on a document without the back story does nothing other than give the opportunity to deny opportunity. Further to that, once the decision has been taken that a person is fit to study/practice then that should be the last time they need to disclose such information. The forced re-living/telling of a part of your life that may well be many years ago and feel as if it belongs to another time can be a traumatic experience. It isn't necessary.

I share this story because I now own it. For too long and for too many people, a care story can be written by others and interpreted through a lens of societal stigma and discrimination. I choose to share my story on my terms, in the hope that it helps to change things for the better. There are those in social work who find it difficult to accept or talk about lived experience with a colleague, they would rather it wasn't mentioned or deem it irrelevant. Some find it wrong that people with experience can practice. There needs to be a peer-led training programme with lived experience at the very heart of delivery. This should be taught at all Universities. Every social worker should learn that care experience is no barrier to anything. I have often said, if you are not looking at someone you support and considering that they could – in other circumstances – be your colleague, then you are not considering their intrinsic value. You are othering them. Should any social work team or University wish to have such insight, and share in the learning journey, then do not hesitate to get in touch.

Hidden oppression

- Laura Bye

An honest disclosure of being care experienced. To begin, I would like to state that I chose this profession as a result of my experiences as a child with corporate parents. I wanted to be like the social workers I remembered making a positive difference in my childhood. Those small things they did and said had the biggest impacts on my life, they empowered me, and because of that, I never lost hope. I am where I am today because, despite the oppression and trauma I experienced as a child, human connection, kindness, and understanding from professionals kept that ray of hope shining. This is why I chose to become a social worker.

Due to the stigma linked to children in foster care, as well as the prejudiced and judgmental comments I have heard personally and as a professional, I have always had conflicting feelings about being care experienced. To provide an example, it is comparable to the social work field, where if you don't know what it is like, it is all too easy to judge social workers based on inaccurate information being projected; regrettably, I have come to discover that the social care system is riddled with controversy. For example, what I have witnessed in social work in the last few years makes me question what I will observe when I am fully emerged.

The profession seeks lived experience knowledge and insight because, after all, that is how professional practice is developed through research that implements policies, which are partly shaped from the lives of people with lived experience. However, this is not always the case, and sharing my personal experiences when working with children and families sometimes leads to unfair comments about 'professional boundaries' and 'conflicts of interest' and 'too child focussed' from professionals.

The disparity in opinions between service users and professionals, on the other hand, has astounded me. Service users appear to connect, even if they are unaware of my disclosure; in my professional judgments, this is where the importance of trust, connection and skills kicks in, and then service users' disclosures and conversations flow naturally; however, I have noticed that professionals feel somewhat threatened by these positive interactions with service users; why, when service user feedback highlights good practice and how beneficial such interactions have been? Professionals have observed and criticised care experienced professionals resulting in a barrier to multi-agency collaboration; this is exactly what the professions say not to do in practice.

Based on my observations, I am wondering if certain professionals are the ones erecting hurdles to child protection and the promotion of child-centred, strength-based social work. My comments may heavily focus on the downsides I have noticed, but what I'm trying to get the reader to see is that there is still a lot of opportunity for change within the social work system, and that when agendas do not align, it leads to poor outcomes for those who need support. I have seen great practice from many organisations and professionals, so this is not by any means to disregard such positives (as there are plenty) but it is more about how we can learn to change something that is not talked about. I feel there is a large amount of fear around care experienced professionals talking up and having their voices heard, hence the title hidden oppression.

I have focused on being able to connect with and engage children and families throughout my working life and becoming a social worker. I have learned to become as knowledgeable as possible from some amazing professionals and I have witnessed what I would say is life changing social work, this has inspired me to becoming the most competent social worker I can be. To ensure that I am equipped to be a highly skilled professional I have undertaken additional training and continued CPD to enable me to build good professional working relationships that improve outcomes. Some professionals have viewed this as priceless, and my practice and dedication to the profession have been appreciated. However, I have found and heard, not just against myself but also from many other care experienced professionals, that having lived experience has been viewed as a negative, and this has oppressed us not only as professionals but has also discriminated against us due to childhood experiences that were out of our control.

These events have caused me to reconsider my decision to pursue a career as a social worker. However, what I have realised is the social work field need people like me, because I am passionate, highly skilled, driven and have the abilities to be an amazing social worker. I can see it is going to be difficult to stay in a profession that is so judgmental, and this has made me have the impression that some professionals do not want to end oppression, social injustice or discrimination. On the other hand, we have professionals who fight so hard to end such obstacles, so how do we get to a line where we are all practicing in an empowering way?

As stated in professional standards and core social work values and ethics, 'care experienced' individuals should be empowered to the highest of standards; however, this does not always happen in the profession, if some professionals cannot do this to professionals who are educated to the same level as them and try to oppress them as professionals by exploiting their vulnerability. Then how can we re-educate?

My points mentioned above are from personal experiences where I am trying to understand where some professionals get their knowledge, as it is does not align with professional codes, values, and standards. Oppression will result in service user dissociation and poor outcomes. Why is this still happening in the field of social work, when we should certainly be learning from serious case reviews? As we all know misused power, can be dangerous and more costly.

I joined the profession to minimise and wishful thinking, but to dismantle such injustices, challenge discrimination, and be a person who can be the voice for people who need it. One person's kindness can truly save lives. However, I may have to do so at the expense of my own mental health or by concealing my identity as care experienced. Now, how can I safely work in a profession that is supposed to promote diversity, equality, and anti-oppressive, anti-discriminatory practice, when some of the professionals in the profession are exhibiting this behaviour?

I ask you this question could it be hidden oppression in the profession, what are your first thoughts when it comes to care experienced professionals?

Title: Don't Judge a Book by its Cover (or by its first chapter)

- Karin Heber

I have never shared this part of me with my colleagues or managers nor with the people I worked with, and I have been a social worker for over 20 years. Since I have a lot of social worker friends hardly any of them know about it either. I often notice my friends and social work colleagues viewing people through the sole lens of their past experiences confirming my beliefs that I would regret sharing this about me. Every action or comment is judged on the back of an assumed past experience of that person. You cannot make mistakes like any other person, but according to them you are making the mistake because of what you have been through. Even achievements are always brought into connection with that.

I want to be seen as me.

I don't see myself as a "victim" or a "survivor" but just judged in relation to my past experiences and that is why I never share this information. If I make a stupid remark or do something wrong, it is not because I was in care, but it is because I am simply a human being with flaws like everybody else.

I would hate to be reduced to being care-experienced, over which I had no control. I want to be judged on the things I had or have control over.

I have never shared it with the people I worked with and lots of them were children and young people in care. I had moments when I was close to sharing because I thought it might help that young person but then I thought their experience is theirs and I just want to focus on that. It felt like diverting the spotlight from them by sharing it.

I never tell employers or managers as I do not want to be exploited for it either.

It is my story to share if I want to, not theirs to exploit to make them look better: "Look at us being so inclusive and supportive - we have lived experience amongst our employees". I also do not want to get a job offered because of that. I am fully aware that this is just me and a lot of others would appreciate a helping hand. I also recognise that I have been quite fortunate as I am reasonably intelligent, had a good education and always great friends who made me feel loved and cherished which made up for the crap family experience. All those things had a major impact on me being able to thrive.

One day (13th February I remember it well) the head teacher took me out of my class which was unheard of unless you were in big trouble. He told me that there was this social worker who would take me home to pack my belongings and would take me and my siblings into care. Off we drove in her car to our house where we, supervised by the social worker and in the presence of our crying mother, packed some things and were taken to foster carers I had never met before. It was far away from where we lived in a tiny rural village so none of my friends could visit nor I them. The only good thing was that I was allowed to remain in my school which was over an hour bus journey away. Our foster carers kept producing children (3 by the time we left) and my siblings and I were handy unpaid nannies and cleaners - it was not optional. They also had big grounds with horses that needed feeding which meant getting up at 5am for us city kids before leaving at 6.30am for our long journey to school. I was never allowed time for my school work as the list of chores was too long, so I tried to do as much work as possible on the bus journey, however, my grades suffered considerably. We also weren't allowed to be in our rooms during the day not that there was much time for it anyway.

The physical abuse by our foster parents did not happen often, and I remember that I always thought I had some superpowers that allowed me to not feel any pain when being hit which was a surprisingly successful technique. The emotional abuse was more scarring. It meant that my siblings and I were played against each other. Our foster parents always chose one of us to be the "bad one" who got all the blame and punishment. We always tried to avoid getting scapegoated by making ourselves look better than the other one. I found it hard to forgive myself for not standing by my brother or sister whenever they were scapegoated, and they had that bad spot far more often than I did.

Our social worker did not know about any of that but then she never asked. I assume she was quite chuffed with herself for having found a placement for us three where we could stay together, even with nice horses and a big garden to play in. The big garden, house and horses just meant lots of work for us as they needed maintaining. Who would pay for that when there is free foster children labour at hand?

I was in foster care with my siblings for 2 years and then my sister and I voted with our feet and refused to go back after a home visit. My little brother had been sent to residential care by that time already. I was 15 years old, and my mother was sober at the time so social services let my sister and I remain there. Foster care certainly is not something to look back on fondly for us. I think even more traumatising for my brother and sister. And for the life of me I could not tell you the name of my social worker. She was female and had curly hair I think but this should tell you about the relationship we had with her. It was not close.

This certainly was the driver for me to enter a career in social work to make this a better experience for others. This and the fact that I have no major talents other than being good with people.

However, the lasting impact on me or biggest damage was not my experience in care but the time before and after (you may have guessed but my mother relapsed pretty quickly). Having a mother with major mental health issues and a severe alcohol addiction and a father who simply did not have an interest in his children other than to feel sorry for him as clearly, he was the victim in all this. Even though my mother was the one showing the bruises and black eyes and we children the ones without proper food or appropriate clothes...

The memories that still hurt are those when I was let down by my parents. For example, my first day of school – all by myself because my mother was too drunk to move never mind accompanying me to school and my father was too busy not caring about his own children. I had to ask a boy I knew would be going to the same school whether his parents could take me with them. The school never had such a situation and did not know how to deal with it. I had to stay back to get the list for schoolbooks with the other parents whilst the children were outside to play. Those are the memories that still make me sad. The foster carers do not mean anything to me and for all I know they were trying to do the right thing even though they should never have been allowed to be foster carers, but we all know how difficult it is to find one who takes 3 siblings. In that sense, I feel lucky to have been able to stay with my brother and sister.

Being let down over and over again by my parents whom I loved was hard, but I can see my mother's addiction and mental health issues for what they are – an illness and not a lack of love for her children. My father had no excuse and I decided that I was better off without him in my life.

One night my mother attempted suicide and was sectioned but we went to school in the morning as if nothing happened. We didn't tell anyone because we were worried that we would be accommodated again without having an adult in the house (my father had left us at this point). We kept our mouths shut and smiled. We kept looking after ourselves which we had always done anyway.

I always insisted on meeting at my friends' rather than at mine as you never knew in what state my mother was in. It would have embarrassed me tremendously for others to see my mother being drunk as none of my friends had problems like that (middle-class families). I've been working since I was 13yrs old (babysitting, farm helper, paper rounds etc) so I had my own money to buy food or stuff I needed for school.

I don't find it difficult to keep this part of me to myself, as I have always led this double life. Nobody knew how bad things were at home or at the foster placement. I did not want this to leak into my happy life with my friends, at school or university so I just put on a smiley face and did not say anything. I left that behind when being in my other life - the one I was in control of. I am happy to say that I live now only one mostly happy life but that is because I keep the lid on my past.

I do not identify as a care-experienced social worker as it reduces my childhood experience to just that - in care - and cuts out all the other bits, good or bad. I am a social worker who had a difficult childhood, but despite all that (not just the being in care), I do not let it define my life. I am in control now and am the person I want to be. I needed to care for myself since I was quite little and am therefore very independent and get things done. I adapt easily and am not shaken by major challenges. So, there are positives to take away from it.

The message I want to give to colleagues is do not reduce people to simply a result of their past experiences because it is not that simple and multiple factors are at play. See them for who they are. I find it insulting if people say: "Isn't it amazing how far you've come given what you have experienced!". I know it is meant well but I have come far simply because I worked hard for it and because I am good at what I do, and I want to have the recognition - if you want to give me one - for that. Also, do recognise the potential importance of other people like brothers, sisters, and friends as they can have a major impact on someone's resilience and self-esteem.

I am the person I am now because of the fantastic people I have had in my life: my sister and brother, my friends, and my boyfriends (former and current) who made me feel loved and worthy of it which made all the difference.

You don't know what it feels like...

- Anon

"You don't know what it feels like to be in care..." A phrase that I hear all the time from the young people in care who I have been the social worker for or have worked with as part of their network of professionals. I find that young people who are in the care of the Local Authority often feel misunderstood and rather 'alone' in their experience of being in care. Especially when adults who are working with them are seen to be making decisions about very sensitive areas of their lives, and from their perspective without a concept of how it might feel for them or how to best help, young people feel that there is real empathy and understanding there.

Little do they know I know exactly how it feels to be in care. Of course, each young person has their individual care experience, and this is unique to them so as a 'care leaver' it would be wrong of me to assume my experience is exactly the same. But the commonality of having lived without biological parents as the main carer is definitely there amongst other things that more often than not being in care comes with. I don't often share that I have care experience with the individuals who I have been the social worker for and more often than not it's an unknown commonality to them. But for myself as a social worker I am able to draw upon my personal experiences of care and have a deep understanding. It is helpful I feel as I have a dual perspective that I know I can draw upon.

I know how it feels to be pulled out of lessons for meetings and for other young people to ask questions and that is why I always ask young people if that's what they want and help them with answers when other young people ask why they are going to meetings or who is that picking you up from school? Often young people are surprised that I have a number of phrases to divert other young people so readily available!

I know how it feels to be labelled as the 'child in care' in school and to have others having lower expectations of me in education due to the statistics that children in care do not perform as well academically in school in comparison to their peers. With a degree, a previous honorary lecturer title, publications, and a peer reviewed research paper amongst other achievements out there I can confidently know that children in care do go on to achieve in education if they have the correct support as I was gratefully able to receive. This has made me a fierce advocate for young people in education and like with any young person they should be supported to achieve their absolute potential in education and in all aspects of their life despite their care experience.

I know how it feels to have to move homes and to move schools, to lose friends, to lose family and to lose belongings. Stability is so important I think many would feel unsettled to be uprooted from everything they know and to be expected to perform life as normal after a short time so I always ask how can we make this move less disruptive? How can we support young people to maintain the relationships that they have formed and how can we ensure that they restore the positive memories of the past?

I know how it feels to feel embarrassed but also protective of birth families and relatives. When young people are feeling conflict, I can help to name the emotions for them, and this helps. Not something I believe every social worker can do as without care experience this might be alien. But there may be something there from personal experience that can relate to this.

I understand the conflict between loving carers or guardians as well as biological family and I know this is a difficult feeling to feel and to talk about, young people have been surprised by the empathy I have for this, yet they don't know why or how I know so much. Never underestimate the honour that you have if a child who you work with is able to allow their barrier down and to really connect with you. This will have been unimaginably difficult for them to allow you in so don't break trust and treasure that. This goes for all professionals.

I know how it feels to feel unworthy. When children sabotage good times and new things, I have felt that and done the same. I can help them to process why they may be doing this and feeling this way and help them to feel worthy. Most children in care feel unworthy in so many ways to the point of questioning why would anyone love me? My own Mum and Dad struggled or so it seemed...

I have deeper level of empathy having been in care. This really helps me, and I am grateful for it. Without my own care experience many of the young people who I have worked with may not have benefited from working with an adult who really does understand and know what it feels like to be in care.

Without a doubt, my care experience shapes my practice, and I am proud that something positive and hopefully helpful has been born from my earlier childhood experiences that for me were so negative.

Does not having care experience disadvantage other social workers? Absolutely not. There are a number of experiences that young people will have and there are many that I have not yet experienced myself but as a practitioner it is important that we reflect and draw upon our own experiences to remember how a particular situation felt for us. We can use our own experiences as well as the tools we have as social workers such as research, direct work and so on in combination to ensure empathy and understanding is always there when we are working with individuals.

Ultimately, we are all human and having empathy is something that I think is at the core of all social work. Not being afraid to share some of ourselves with the individuals we work with whilst being mindful that we absolutely maintain our professional boundaries (keeping in mind that our own experiences that have shaped us) can also help in social work practice.

What I would add is that for care leavers going into social work, especially, it is important to be mindful of triggers and work that may feel 'close to home' like with any level of trauma people in general need to be very self-aware and have the confidence to raise when a piece of work is likely to be too sensitive. This applies to all social workers and their own lived experiences too. Self-care should not be underestimated, especially for those who come into social work having experienced, for example, trauma or abuse in any form as there will be challenges and in order to support others, we must ensure our own self care is also catered for.

Unseen: Reflections of a Black Care Experienced Foster Child

- Rebecca Olayinka

I remember that I had wanted to be a counselling psychologist, (not a social worker) but my grasp of mathematics wasn't strong enough to do the master's course that I wanted, so I figured social work was the next best thing. I had a strong desire to help people and I felt that I was a resourceful and independent type of person so I could use my skills to do exactly that.

I hated seeing people in pain and suffering and if I could help then I would do my best. When I was a child and sometimes as a young adult I would cry when I saw others in pain, it was like I was feeling their feelings through me! Empathy is one of my strengths however I aim to be more balanced with this as at times it can make you procrastinate on decisions as worrying about what others may feel about these decisions.

I never really thought that my upbringing was tied to my decision to be a social worker and my negative experiences of social services in my childhood and that I wanted to re-frame that experience by being able to help others even though I wasn't helped.

I went through most of my degree, still oblivious to what was underneath my decision. I had a breakdown during my third-year placement and for some reason all the stuff from my childhood came roaring to the surface spilling out like a volcano that had just erupted. They say "what you resist persists "this was so true for me.

I had confided in one of the practitioners on placement and she was worried about me so told her superiors and that was the end of that. I was signed off sick and even when I was better and cleared by Occupational Health I still wasn't allowed to return.

Yet I persevered with my degree and my next placement was a success, my practice teacher was very knowledgeable and the experience I got there, helped me to land a job really quickly after I qualified. All in all, it worked out well, but it could have been very different. There was no real support in terms of being care experienced and doing a social work degree. If there was further support in place from universities and placement settings it would have been much more beneficial for myself and other students who had similar experiences. I realise it is up to us as professionals to change the ways in which we support care experienced students and when they become professionals possibly through coaching and mentoring and peer support groups particularly if they may have had slightly unconventional roads within the fostering system.

I acknowledge that it took me sooo long to own that I was care experienced, in particular a Black care experienced child. It felt like a dirty word, like a bad taste that I couldn't ever get out of my mouth. I also felt that as I was privately fostered that I wasn't "really fostered".

I wasn't able to speak about it, because my mother did not wish to talk about it and so I felt silenced for many, many years. That is slowly changing and writing this piece is testimony of that.

My own experiences of being a Black foster child, which was slightly unconventional to the fostering system as a whole as I was firstly – privately fostered and secondly both my mother and father who were of Nigerian origin, but they were both in the UK when I was fostered.

I was the last of their 4 surviving children. I had an older brother and sister, but they died before I was born. My older sister (my closest sibling in age and proximity) was fostered too but we were fostered at different times and being 7 years her junior, it didn't exactly help build our bond and it is something that we are continuing to work on as adults as we grew up like only children.

Private fostering is not uncommon in the Black Community. I was privately fostered from the ages of 0-9.5, my formative years. There was a surge in private fostering particularly in the Nigerian community from the 1980's and is still ongoing, remember the tragic short life of Victoria Climbié?

For those who may not be familiar with private fostering it is defined in Section 66 (1a 1b) of the Children Act 1989.

"A Privately fostered child" means a child who is under the age of sixteen and who is cared for, and provided with accommodation in their own home by, someone other than a parent of his; a person who is not a parent of his but who has parental responsibility for him; or a relative of his; and to foster a child privately means to look after the child in circumstances in which he is a privately fostered child as defined by this section"

From my own experiences of being in the care system and what I still witness today. I have become increasingly aware that as a society we do not speak about black foster children. We speak about care leavers; however, the majority of conversations are focused on those who are from a white background, which begs the questions if black foster children are forgotten by society? Or do we just not recognise black children as first and foremost children? But see them as adults before their time? There are more studies into this phenomenon coined; adultification.

''Adultification is a form of dehumanization, robbing black children of the very essence of what makes childhood distinct from all other developmental periods: innocence." (Casey, 2017)

More on Adultification, specific to Black girls, can be found in The Casey-funded report 2017 Girlhood Interrupted: The Erasure of Black Girls' Childhood, discovered that adults viewed black girls "as less innocent and more adult-like than white girls of the same age, especially between 5–14 years old." (Casey 2017)

Looking back, I am not sure if I was viewed more as an adult during my childhood years, but I wonder if that's why I didn't get much help? I was definitely treated differently, and this was due to my race and the unconscious biases that played out. I also felt that being Black and care experienced put me in different worlds that I couldn't really navigate.

I was Black, female, child and care experienced. These all have layered complexities with just one of these adjectives, let alone put together. Looking back, I do think that the weight was a lot to carry for so young a person.

My foster mother was a white woman called Mummy Marceline. We lived in a small town called Clacton-on-Sea about 40 minutes outside London, and within the town we were situated in an even smaller rural village called Jaywick Sands.

The beach was only a stone's throw away and was the highlight of my time there and being able to play with my friends. I felt free despite the incessant racism that I plagued me on an almost daily basis.

I remember having children who would at first play games with me and then if I won or I did something they didn't like, they would band together to inflict an onslaught of verbal racist abuse towards me.

I usually came in crying to Mummy Marceline who would give me names and insults to hail back at them for equal measure. Mummy M would reassure me that it was the children who had the problem not me. At times she would come out and speak to them, but it was to no avail as they didn't listen.

I longed to be part of a group and a community as it was at times very isolating with just me and Mummy Marceline. I had two best friends: Kimberly and Tina. They were perhaps my only friends. Kimberly's mum and Mummy Marceline were best friends, and I never felt any different when I was with Kimberly and her family and often stayed over at Kimberly's house and she at mine.

My relationship with Tina however at times mimicked the relationship I had with the children who I used to play games within my area. One minute it was friendly the next it was fraught where there was a lot of racial abuse hurled my way. I gave as good as I got, but I did wonder if we were truly friends? Tina's mum also did not like me and for a long time Mummy M did not want me to be friends with Tina due to her mother not liking me. Her mother did come round in the end, but I never knew what prompted the change. It wasn't the same relationship I had with Kimberly's family, but Tina's mum was more accommodating, and I could go round Tina's house sometimes.

I was seen only twice by two different social workers in the whole time I was there. They were both middle class white women, who if I didn't know any better could be twins. They were appointed only when the hot subject of whom I was going to permanently live came to ahead, Mummy Marceline or my mother? My mother wanted me back and Mummy Marceline wanted me to stay. It seems that there was not much interest in me before that even though there were no other black children in my area, and I had a white older woman whom everyone knew looked after me. I didn't seem to be given much thought, even though the duty of the local authority is defined in Section 67 (1) (2 a) of the Children Act 1989 as follows.

"It is the duty of the local authority to satisfy themselves that the welfare of children privately fostered in their area are safeguarded and that an officer of the local authority should visit in prescribed circumstances and on specific occasions within specified periods."

I did not receive such attention and it is no wonder that I am still working on getting whatever files I did have from my local authority who thinks these have now been destroyed yet provides me with the same old response. I knew it happened I have pictures and family members who remember also.

From these experiences, I can see why black foster children can feel forgotten, abandoned and neglected not only by their birth family but by the state as well.

My separation from my foster mother was in essence; traumatic. I was forced to go kicking and screaming against my will as my mother had decided she wanted me back with her to live in London. When I went back to live with my mother, there was no support available, and I ended up having a fraught relationship with my mother that sadly never reconciled as it will be 14 years in November 2022 since she passed away.

My foster mother died a few months after I had been taken from her. Social care did not want to know they were probably just relieved I was back with my mother, and it was one less case for them to manage, one less child, or should I say (black child) in their care.

I became an angry and confused young child. Living back with my mother was vastly different, I needed to get used to a new culture and a new way of living. On one hand it was positive that I did not have the racism that I endure when living with Mummy Marceline, yet I didn't have my friends and had very little resemblance of who I was before.

 My mother still wasn't really in the right frame of health to care for me, so I had to do a lot for myself from a very young age like make my own dinner and wash my clothes, even had to use my pocket money to buy underwear, we were also on the breadline and our house was in a state of poverty for years.

Since my mother was physically ill most of the time, I felt forced to care for her. This at the time made me resent her more as I was the child. I felt my childhood ended the day I got taken away from Mummy Marceline and even though I cried about it, not knowing I was mourning a childhood that I no longer had, there was nothing I could do. No one seemed to care.

I had always thought I was Brown and not Black, and this led to bullying and social exclusion at my new primary school as I was not perceived as knowing my identity. In truth I didn't.

I didn't know if I was Brown or Black, I didn't know if I was British or Nigerian, or both. I didn't know where I belonged and where home really was. Mummy Marceline's was never a permanent place as fostering essentially is not. Yet without the comfort of her presence, I really felt forgotten, not knowing who I was or who my family was really and them also not knowing me either.

The issue I had continued long into my adult years, before I became a qualified as a social worker and sometime afterward. Being a social worker gave me the access to develop my skills self-awareness and reflective skills, yet my own story felt like it was a constant shadow following me wherever I went, yet the more I talk about it the more it has helped. I feel that being care experienced has informed my practice as even though I worked in adult care I always been curious about someone's background, particularly if there were safeguarding issues involved and I have at times found that people with very complex lives have usually been care experienced. I have always been very keen on being a person-centred practitioner and maybe it's because for a long time particularly as a child, I didn't feel listened to or felt that I had a voice and I know first-hand how difficult that can be.

My decision to help others kept me going, yet I needed a lot of help myself and it felt like I was on a very lost and lonely path. I didn't really have a functional family and I just partied a lot to feel that never ending void that I was scared to touch, so I just kept running away from it all. It wasn't just about who I was, it was about what I had been through and not understanding why I had multiple periods of depression and anxiety and that sometimes just functioning day to day was too much and many times questioned the reason for my existence.

Living a life of not feeling loved so I didn't love myself, I felt that love was part of my childhood with Mummy Marceline and after that it had forsaken me for greener pastures.

I didn't realise for a very long time that love was still a part of me, it hadn't left me, it was still with me. As I write these words, I become a little emotional. Thinking about Mummy Marceline and my mother. It is funny how you can miss a person after they have been deceased for many years.

Time heals but it never forgets. That is one of the reasons I started writing. I saw writing as 'my fighting' a way to deal with all the emotional turmoil that I had. The rejection, the pain, the feelings of disdain from myself and what I perceived from others.

Times are changing, but I'm not sure if it's quick enough. I don't want people to go through what I went through. The burden of shame and guilt can be heavy and weigh down on my heart for far too long. Long after my fostering journey ended, I always felt on the outside looking in, a prisoner in a sea of shame, although it was never my shame, I just believed that it was all the same.

I believed my life ended when I left Mummy Marceline yet, it was ongoing, it was just a plot twist of my story it isn't finished. I can continue to create new beginnings for myself and help other people, particularly Black experienced foster children. As Black experienced children may feel that they are forgotten in the UK and face multiple levels of disadvantages and oppression in society. So, I want to use my to voice support them to create a future of no limit or bounds and one that's of their own creation, regardless of what has happened in the past.

Casey, A. (2017) New Study: The "Adultification" of Black Girls. [Blog] Available at; New Study: The "Adultification" of Black Girls - The Annie E. Casey Foundation (aecf.org) [Accessed 06/10/2021]

REFLECTIONS

We can shift things through our actions

- Naz

It is so easy to be labelled today, either by society or other professionals. One of the labels which has followed me through the years was the label of being a care leaver. Undeniably although the label had offered me a multitude of opportunity with the local authorities, or charities and other agencies: it highlights one of the very vulnerabilities that young people deal with. Often young people won't even acknowledge such a title as it is a reminder of a traumatic ordeal.

I experienced such a phase growing up, there were times I really struggled with my own identity, not only was I care leaver, but I also had the stigma of growing up with a physical disability as well as developing a hidden disability which manifested from my early teens into my adulthood in the shape of my mental health.

Often at times, I struggled with my religious values as well as western society norms. Nothing seemed to come with ease, there were constant opportunities which were missed and barriers I had to face. I developed 'people pleasing' behaviours and started to lose my own identity in the process. I could differentiate between what was morally right and wrong but struggled with what was right for me and what direction my life will take.

Growing up in care, was a challenge. I was surrounded by young people who had dealt with severe trauma and processed their feelings through drugs, alcohol, or explicit demeanour. There was a pressure to fit in and I would spend most evenings feeling isolated. I studied hard and focused all my energy on my education, I developed a passion for the arts and found a way that helped me articulate myself. There were moments I felt very alone, to fill the void within me I would speak to the support workers on site in the care home because during those times, my social worker always made it a point to say she was always busy. I felt as though I couldn't open or speak of my feelings. I wasn't aware of where to get help or who I could go to.

I remember a vivid memory of living in an assessment unit, it was called Fairfield. I was only supposed to be there for 6 weeks but because of how social services passed my case around, I resided there for an entire year until I was put in a hostel which was quite traumatic. Suddenly, I was expected to know how benefits worked, how to pay rent and just survive at the tender age of 17. This assessment unit helped shape some of my beliefs and encouraged independence in a variety of ways. I remember going into the manager's office late in the evening and requesting money for a scientific calculator so I could complete my A level assignments and I remember the manager of the unit just smiling at me. In that moment she put her work away and called me near to her desk and we started looking at online stores to purchase my own calculator. I remember feeling happy. This was probably the first time I went to a professional and they listened. During the period of the year, the workers in Fairfield's got to know me, they respected me as a person and albeit I was just a child they treated me as a young adult, culpable and responsible for my own decisions. The support workers aided me more than my social workers. I remember they purchased my first smart phone so I could call for emergencies. Initially going to school on public transport was scary but they really built my confidence up so I could engage in independent tasks. I wasn't exposed to such independence in my family home, I lived a sheltered life.

Although I was surrounded by challenging environments, it was during those moments I visited some fond memories of my childhood. My parents and siblings always encouraged the idea that knowledge is key and thus one should focus on education. Both my parents came to England with little to no knowledge of the English language. Mum would describe her experience in England as oppressive because she was unable to access support, she wasn't aware of how to access education and she felt frustrated that she could not provide support for her children at times. Growing up, although the decline of my mother's mental health had significant impact in my upbringing, it made me aware of the lack of social support available for parents who immigrated into this country. If some of these concerns were addressed perhaps my childhood experience would have been significantly different. Perhaps it would've prevented me from going into care. If a whole family approach was adopted within my family perhaps there would have been more of an incline of keeping the family together.

When I left care and went into a hostel, that was difficult because as well as trying to survive on the limited benefits, I was trying to complete my A-levels and worked a night job to support myself. It was during this phase of my life, the pressure started to take a toll on me, talking to professionals was difficult because when I was growing up in the system I felt as though no one listened to me, one year I didn't even see my social worker. It shook my faith in the system, and it embedded this idea of survival. It was only when I was transferred into the care-leavers team I saw significant improvements in my well-being. My personal advisor was the only professional who really worked with me as opposed to working against me. She would see me regularly.

At first when I was introduced to personal advisor, I was only 16 years old and I had made a judgment based on the previous professionals that worked with me. However, I can honestly say if it wasn't for my personal advisor, I probably would not be the person I am today. She encouraged me to grow personally as well as professionally. Encouraged confidence within me and I was able to live abroad to complete my undergrad studies and she motivated and inspired me to apply for a job as employability case manager working for a charity call CGL (Change Grow Live), supporting young care leavers to get into education, training, or employment. She saw something in me that I couldn't see for myself, and it was through this employment and conversations with my personal advisor. I was inspired to study MA social work. I wanted to inspire vulnerable children and families the same way my personal advisor had inspired me and helped me understand that our past experiences define the people we become today and develop into tomorrow. As humans we will make mistakes, but we learn from them thus every experience we face in life, albeit it maybe challenging, offers a learning opportunity.

Studying my master's in social work now, made me realise the multiple complexities social workers face, the pressure, the workload. It is demanding but rewarding. My experience in care has helped inform my social work practice. For an example: during placement it was important for me to introduce myself to the children and families. Make face to face contact and engage in direct work to build a rapport because this was something I didn't receive from my early care experience which resulted in my lack of trust in professionals and burdening myself. Taking a strength based, or relation-based approach seems to be quite prevalent in my own practice. I feel it's important to highlight the things that are going well amongst chaos in the lives of vulnerable people.

There were challenging moments, and I would find myself overwhelmed at times, some of the children and young people who were allocated to me had so many complexities which surrounded them - it was difficult prioritising which concern should be addressed. However, in those moments I received support from my Practice Educator as well as my Academic Tutor who helped me navigate through the concerns and understand the needs of the clients and helped me prioritise my own wellbeing as well.

Using Vygotsky's zone of proximal development, I was able to identify the things I can do; what can I do with support as well as understanding the limitations of the role. For an example: in placement I was able to engage in tasks and attend meetings knowing I was able to manage my anxieties through the right preparation materials put in place. During difficult times there were moments where I felt overwhelmed. However, placement is a learning environment, and it offers the opportunity for us to grow professionally as practitioners.

Social work is ever evolving, there are different approaches being used but as a student with care experience I feel as though taking an empathetic approach towards the children, families, and adults we work with is a key component. I have seen other social workers and agencies in professional capacities not engage with children or families directly. They merely fill out documents on behalf of the children and families because of the high demand but it is important to build relationships because they will be times where the only support that child or family might have will be us (the social workers). We can either inspire change through support or create mistrust because we have not taken the time to understand or build a rapport with clients. The very power dynamic can be shifted through our actions, and it is important to recognise that.

Shaking of the shame

- Marie

I knew I was going to be a social worker pretty much as soon as social workers became involved in my life. The moment I was taken into care was truly awful. I was taken out of school and taken to the social work office. From here, a social worker who I didn't know came in to see me twice in four hours. (I now understand they were looking for a placement for me whilst likely tending to other immediate tasks). I was taken to my first ever placement by two social workers who complained the entire way about having to work late. One social worker couldn't put her children to bed. I felt ashamed that two strangers had to look after me that night. I felt guilty.

In my careers class just a few weeks after entering care, I asked how I can become a social worker.

'You should look at other careers.'

'No, I'm going to be a social worker.'

My tutor laughed and told me no one he knows grows up to do the job they set out to do. In some instances, he was right. Prior to wanting to become a social worker, I was intent on becoming a web designer. I paid so much attention to the intricacies of website design and begged my teacher Mr Singh at the time to teach me more in lunchtimes. Then my life changed. I left home to go to school one day and then I never returned home again. In fact, I never saw my family ever again. To this day, I have only seen my mother on one occasion before her death. From this day forward, I didn't have a home. I had a placement, and I had a career. I had people who cared about me, but they didn't love me. I had people who hugged me but only from the side. I had a family who loved me but from afar.

My experiences were painful, and a lot were made more painful by a painful system. I knew there was no damn way I was going to let other children feel the way I was made to feel. As a child, I was invited to take part in my meetings but only after professionals had spoken about me for 45 minutes. The meeting was over before I even walked in. I was begged to come downstairs so my social worker could ask me the same 5 questions she asked me every 6 weeks. I listened to social workers moan about working late again. I was constantly told my placement was at risk and that I was causing a lot of stress to those around me. No one ever acknowledged that I'd lost my whole family in an instant. Yes, on paper there were severe problems in my family, but they were still my family. My family became a topic to brush over in meetings. No contact. Next.

So, I vowed I'd become a social worker and I did. I've been a social worker for six years now. I'm extremely proud and I know that good social work, even in one interaction, can have the most positive impact. But I wonder if I've become the social worker I vowed to be all those years ago.

As I sit here writing this, I know in some instances I'm not. That very shame I felt as a 12-year-old still sits with 30-year-old me. I'd go to school and work as hard as possible not to share my care experienced status. I'd make up fake parents and aunties. I'd explain my mum was sick which is why my family friend was at the school play. When I made it to university, I thought that the shame would be behind me; I'm on a level playing field. The truth is you're not. I still had to fit into a largely middle-class world I wasn't part of. At least at first. The shame did ease a little bit though. I realised that lots of people come from complicated backgrounds, and I felt safe to share some of my history as I made relationships and grew more linked to the middle class world I was now part of.

Eventually, I became a social worker. My dream. At this point, I thought everything really was behind me. There would be no shame. I'd work with people who understood me and in turn I'd support others to feel a little more understood. Except, it didn't quite work like that.

I suddenly sat in two worlds. My friends who I met in care were horrified. Suddenly, they didn't want to confide in me about their children or life anymore. I remember my best friend saying, 'oh no, you've become one of them'. Her voice was filled with true horror. I realised I was causing fear in my friends although nothing had changed. Friends told me about their traumatic experience of social workers, and I felt a traitor. I was apologising on behalf of the profession I was now a part of. I wondered why I'd decided to become one of the people who hurt me so much? Why didn't I sit with the anger my friends did? I tried not to mention my social work status around friends too much. I was ashamed.

When I started my first day as a newly qualified social worker, I was so excited. I had made it. I was about to begin working in a tough London council and I was going to make a difference. I value deeply some of the wonderful colleagues I met in my role but the shame that I had been working so hard to pat down returned with a vengeance. Instead of being open about my own history, I resorted back to my 12-year-old self with a fake family, life and history. I pretended not to know terms relating to children looked after even though I was far too acquainted with PEPs, medicals and conferences. I didn't want to be found out as I was supposed to be the newly qualified social worker.

I visited children and shuffled as uncomfortably as them when they asked me any personal questions. I imagined what the repercussions would be for me professionally if I was to be honest. I imagined being confronted by Social Work England for having a history they probably wouldn't understand. I imagined the consequences if I was to be honest and say to teenagers, you know what, I was in care too and so I don't actually have the experiences you think I have. I imagined what it would feel for some young people to see that another care experienced person had made something of themselves. But it was always imagination. And young people continued their imagination of my perfect life and deep pockets. I imagined the trouble I would get in for my own family history. It brought shame. I was ashamed. As ashamed as 12-year-old me.

I moved to a new authority some years later and with that I gained some confidence. I started to tell some people about my history for it was part of me. I'd proved myself as a competent social worker and I was now senior. So, I decided to use my power and be upfront and honest with colleagues. Some social workers were wonderful. They cared about me and treated me just as any other. Some were not so wonderful.

When a child I was caring for on my caseload almost died by suicide, I was devastated. Devastated I had not been able to stop this child feeling as I did so many years ago. I'd sacrificed so much to become a social worker. I'd sacrificed my history, my evenings and often my wellbeing. I felt the pain of that young person. I couldn't function. I cared about this young person. I really cared.

Some days later, a senior member of management came in to tell me he was worried about me. He came to tell me I hadn't processed my own experiences and maybe I should see if I could afford therapy and attend the gym too. My response of sadness was irrational. I sat there absolutely gob smacked and resorted to my 12-year-old self, agreeing and willing them to leave me alone. I felt shame. Shame for caring. Shame for not shrugging off an almost suicide. Shame for showing sadness. Shame for not being as tough as every other social worker.

It was then I realised that I didn't quite fit into the social work world or the care experienced world. My care experienced friends feared me. My young people thought I was posh. My social work colleagues thought I was there to solve my own past or simply couldn't believe I was care experienced without serious personal difficulties. When out with friends, if anyone asked me my job, I'd just explain 'I work for the council'. Everywhere I went, I carried shame.

This is the thing. I'm 30 years old now and my care experience is still a massive part of my identity. It illustrates my life. Conversations about family, Christmas traditions, money, just about everything is interrupted by my care experience. In social work, we fight for life to feel a little fairer, but it was my social work colleagues who sometimes made me feel like life was very unfair. Colleagues who as adults made me feel as I did as a child. But there were also some similarities. I had some lovely social workers as a child. One is now a dear friend. As an adult, some of my social work colleagues have embraced, loved and appreciated me. Some are now my dear friends. I care for them as deeply as they care for me. Those colleagues bring me warmth and help to bring down that shame. I hold onto that.

Identity Conflict

- Victoria-Maria

As a foster child, I often felt frustrated with the lack of opportunities I was given to speak out regarding decision making, - especially as some of the decisions made by social workers had detrimental consequences upon my wellbeing. These feelings of frustration re-emerged whilst I was studying for my social work degree during the Coronavirus pandemic, and global restrictions were introduced. I channelled my frustrations by adopting new advocacy roles for students, including care leavers at the university. My actions were complimentary to social work standards; however, I had not anticipated these frustrations to impact my practice as much as they did. I recognised I had been driven by the emotions I experienced as a foster child. Unintentionally I had returned to feelings of being unimportant, undervalued and not worthy enough to contribute towards my own life. Only this time, they were powerful and enabling; they did not submissively accept the situation. They challenged it.

But who challenged these restrictions, who fought for the care leavers seemingly forgotten in their university rooms; the student social worker *who challenged* or the foster child *who felt it?*

Whose voice was being listened to?

As I enter my final year of university, I will explore this voice. The foster child will be unearthed, dusted off and given the platform to speak. However, I, the student social worker, will provide her with the microphone.

Are you listening?

It Wasn't OK Little One

- Victoria-Maria

My 16th birthday came and gifted me independence. Conversations of me leaving foster care had circulated for months prior, and I was exhausted. The foster care system had drained me. Almost every week was filled with the terrain of unpredictable introductions and broken night's sleep as Emergency Protection Orders were issued during the night. I would hear little legs scramble up the side of my bunk bed, scurry up against the wall as their sobbing eventually offered them the sanctuary of sleep.

It's ok, little one. This room is yours as well now.

I was introduced to new household members as their 'foster sister' before I learned their names. We would talk about how long we have lived in the house with the other foster children, competing against one another for acceptance from the carers. I would welcome new faces and listen to their trauma and the stories that have brought them to my room.

It's ok, little one. I hear you.

I was exhausted from being constantly alert, always having to know where my belongings were. I had learned to limit my belongings to a pile of clothes and a makeup bag that would fit snugly in a Reebok gym bag. The thought of leaving my bag in the hallway or even just on the living room floor was quite thrilling. My belongings followed me everywhere, like a faithful puppy, a tired, beaten puppy.

It's ok, little one. You can rest now.

My feet hurt from walking around new neighbourhoods, trying to remember my way back to my new foster home. Round in circles, looking for familiar houses and gardens that I saw from the back seat of my social workers' car. My lungs ached from holding my breath as I tentatively knocked on the front door, hoping to be greeted with the same face that had spoken to my social worker the night before.

It's ok, little one. It won't hurt anymore.

I ached from shame as I could barely remember how to get back to my new foster home from school, let alone recall the address. 'How can you not know your own address' others would scoff. Once, whilst crying in a payphone, I gestured for a Postman to speak to my foster mum for the address. He walked me to the house.

It's ok, little one. Your home now.

Now I was all grown up at 16 years and four months old; I could live alone and finally have a peaceful night's sleep. My second-hand bed was included in a standard bedroom package bought with a £25 furniture allowance from social services, along with a wardrobe and bedside unit. Darkness comforted me that first night. I felt my way back to my bed and woke to absolute silence.

It's not ok, grown one. You are alone now.

I leaned over the banister to see who was walking up the stairs and decided to interrupt the stranger's path with a handshake – just like the grown-up I now am. I was suspicious of his care leaver title as he was older than me, although only by a year.

It's not ok, grown one. You do not know him.

We settled into one another's routine until they eventually merged. We shared our stories of trauma, reconciling each other whilst recounting childhood experiences. We shared our desires to belong to a family. We shared a bed.

It's not ok, grown one. This is trauma bonding.

The air in the flat was stale, and my stomach grew tight. My fingers were sore from scrubbing my clothes clean in the bath. My clothes would harden against the back of the chair as they dried and were cruel on my skin as I moulded into them. Blood fell to the floor as I misjudged my aim to open a tin of rice pudding. I didn't have a tin opener or a washing machine, but I did have the independence that everyone had upsold me, right?

It's not ok, grown one. This is survival.

My attendance in year 10 was 36%, so it was decided that I would not sit them. I did not decide this. Desperate to gain an education and be given the opportunity to sit my GCSE's I enrolled at college. Now I am *independent*, I can do what I want, and I wanted to study. The books were too expensive for me, and the travel was hard on my legs. My clothes were powder stained where I had not rinsed them properly, and I was lonely at college.

It's not ok, grown one. You have mountains to climb.

The flat grew colder, and my stomach began to grow. I yearned for the belonging I had spoken of whilst thumbing the Argos catalogue cooing over baby items. Packing my faithful Reebok bag, I followed my grief back to my mothers. I no longer had the safety net of foster care to return to; I am 16 now, able to make my own decisions, right?

My mother closed the door behind me.

It's not ok, grown one. You are not safe.

Standing in the shadow of my enemy

- David Grimm

As with all of the other writers in this book, I have my own reasons for applying to become a social worker and undergoing the training. The primary one being that I want to be a better social worker than the ones I was given, I am not saying that they were all of poor calibre, just most of them. With that said, I often reflect on the fact that the training is not easy, it is not for the faint of heart, and it requires what can only be known as a special type of commitment (not to over inflate any of our collective egos). A commitment that many of you reading this will have. But not all. In truth I am convinced on a daily basis, upon any moment of structured thought, that I am both absolutely right for the role and simultaneously the most nuclear and destructive option that could be presented to a person in need of support. To clarify, I don't believe myself a threat or a toxic person, but I have grown up seeing social work as my enemy, the people that would dictate and condone, the people that brought police or took us away from my mum...but not soon enough and not as a sibling unit. The people who applied methods of intervention that directly lead to family disengagement and broken relationships. This leaves me concerned that my past biases of social work will leak into my own practice and impact upon those under my care.

You will undoubtedly have been told to reflect, then reflect some more and reflect upon those reflections (not those words maybe)? We must always be reflecting and being critical of ourselves and practice. As brilliantly put in the words of Siobhan Maclean:

"Reflection isn't just about looking back, it's about thinking all of the time, it's about thinking in the moment, it's about thinking ahead. It's about exploring our feelings; how do we feel about that? What feelings does that invoke in us? It's about connecting things with our emotions" (Maclean, 2020)

In using this thought process to reflect on my wish to "be a better social worker" and my feelings of "me versus social work" I have been trying to crystallise my reasons for joining the social work course (besides the reasons above) and why I have allowed myself to garner aspirations of supporting people. This has been a gruelling slog with much doubt and a lot of question of whether I should even remain on the course. My processing pattern has never been known to be the clearest, and with much of my memory being fuzzy and clouded by fog (years on years of broken and unclear memories) it meant even the Fundamentals like my values, ethics and principles came into play, questioning all of the pillars of my being. The question of my own care experience was always at the forefront of my mind, and whether it would be a detriment to my advocating on behalf of the people in my care, grew to be entirely exhausting, causing me to feel like a self-defeated LAAC (Looked after and accommodated Child). A characteristic I have been fighting, lobbying, and advocating against for more than seventeen years.

If you take nothing else from my writing and reflections, please, take the message that abbreviations and acronyms such as LAAC aren't just hurtful in the way that they make care experienced people feel. These may be morally wrong in the sense that they function as a bureaucratic separation between service and client, the care experienced people in our care are more than numbers, more than acronyms and more than sheets of paper with our scribbled notes, we must never forget this, and you must strive to be better than the previous generation of practitioner, many of whom had never been challenged or shown a different practice.

I used to believe that this was ok, they don't know any better, so they have the right to act and behave however they like, so long as they believed it was in the best interest of the person they were caring for. This has been a detrimental and pervasive attitude I've had internally, that I have been working on for the last several years since I read my residential care notes and started working with Who Cares? Scotland. Challenging all levels of the social work world on their attitudes and practice of record writing. This was also when I started to consider that care is a lifelong event and as such, we must challenge all social workers to have fresh updated practice methods. With the intention that they have less of a chance in accidentally impacting a care experienced person's life in negative way, far after we are gone from their lives. As well as just improving practice. Other than anecdotal and stories from older care experienced people, I hold no evidence of care experience being a lifelong phenomenon and undoubtedly this statement will not apply to all of the care experienced individuals, but it is important for us to constantly explore how we collaborate with the people in our social work care and the ways in which they are thriving or the ways in which they are wilting on the vine.

"Life outcomes for people who spent time in the care of the state as children ('care-experienced') are known to be significantly lower, on average, than for the general population. The reasons for this are complex and multidimensional, relating to social upheaval, disrupted schooling, mental and physical health issues and societal stigmatisation." (Harrison, Baker, Stevenson 2020)

This statement tied closely with many of the negative sentiments I felt upon the reading of my care records, from the authority that had homed me and considering how long I took to enter Higher Education, the statement also rung true, perhaps for me as an individual only but I would doubt this, after listening to tales from older care experienced people and knowing of the similar difficulties we all faced.

In the reading of my records, I found that I had been mis-named, mis-identified and identified as my brother instead of myself, as well as being refused certain files from social work involvement in my life as these were categorised as my mother's files only. Irrespective of the fact that her social worker had, in turn, been involved in my life. This devastating envelope of paper did nothing but encourage my feelings that I had been living my own "David and Goliath" story. Creating a sense that the social work and I were somehow in contention as opposed to championship between us. Even still, even through this feeling of being an enemy of my own caretakers, much to my own disbelief, I found out that I had a reference number - *though looking back now I am unsure why I was so shocked*. We used to joke about this in care, that we were nothing more than a file number to the staff, nothing more than a number that would be forgotten upon expulsion or absentia from care, yet here I was reading my own number. Not a joke, not a myth, a genuine series of digits that had been used to categorise me, and more efficiently than my previous note takers it would seem. A storm of feelings filled with dread, sickness, revelation, and disheartenment all rolled into one and hung over me for days. In one moment, this bureaucratic separation had hit me and lay with me, I tried several times to discuss this feeling but couldn't describe it quite succinctly. Now I will admit, I have never challenged the persons that wrote my files, but as many of you know there are languages that we have accepted in the social work status quo, and I am asking you that you be self-aware and not fall into that trap. It only takes a few of us to make enough noise for change and set an example by stopping doing these behaviours, and we will implement a new status quo for the next generation to embrace, challenge or annihilate. All I can say with absolute certainty, regardless of my daily doubts, is that I LACK (LAAC) for nothing. As is the same for my friends and colleagues throughout this book, and *more importantly* the people you will have supported/go on to support and function as a role model towards.

None of the above will be easy, I embrace this, but all change starts from trying to create a new way of working. I will start from now on when I have those self-defeating doubts by replacing them with the mantra below:

"I am a strong and thriving social work student and I will never again be known as Reference number: S7040912, I am human, I am thriving, and I am an example to someone out there who needs even the slightest bit of inspiration, I exist for a reason, and I will see it come true."

This may seem overly simplistic and borderline dismissive of the pains many care experienced people have been through, this is in no manner my intention and I wish it known that I recognise the pains and empathise also. We all have our shared experience but also have our own bull to take by the horns and conquer. This mantra is merely the best way I can encourage myself to be positive going forwards, and as stated each of us will find a different method for thriving, and as we learn, reflect, and grow, this will become clearer and clearer to you, and you will be the best social worker you can for all those in your care.

In the spirit of learning and growth, I would like us to take a leaf from the writings of Dr Prospera Tedam, given to us in the pages of the Outlanders book:

"As a social work educator and trainer, my philosophy is one where I strive to create an inclusive learning environment for all, where each student or participant is respected and listened to. I have always aimed, through my research to recognise the diverse pathways through which race may influence experiences and outcomes for social workers, service users and students." (Tedam, 2021)

Understandably this was written in a different context to what we are discussing now but is a level of reflective and holistic practice to aspire to. One that I believe will encourage and promote inclusivity regardless of which background the care experienced person has. I would also like to invite all readers to reflect on the following questions and their implications for practice. You can feed your answers back through twitter or keep them private, whether you are a PhD holder, an undergraduate student or a person that has only now developed an interest in social work, how would you answer the following?

- How often do I use acronyms and disembodied language in practice? Why do I do this? and how will I endeavour to adapt this?

- How will I create an inclusive environment for ALL through my practices?

- How will I minimise future harm (mentally, spiritually, or physically) to the people I support?

- And how will I give myself the time and appropriate space for personal reflection?

I ask these questions not to discourage you from practice but rather, to try and enhance the way we ALL think and practice going forward.

So, to highlight, I do not consider each and every social worker I meet to be my enemy. Without an incline of doubt, I consider social workers to be of the very best people I have happened across in life, some of the most considerate, well-meaning, and philanthropically minded people ever. Many of whom have their own challenges and past lives that have driven them to the profession, I am in awe of social workers daily, whether they are students/ ASYE/ interns or they have been leading the field for the last thirty years. I am starstruck by the way they challenge and conquer the endless parade of obstacles that come their way and I will be proud to join these people in the work they do. However, I do hold our system in a bleak and negative view. Whether this has come from twenty-eight years of social work having a role in my life (interventions/rehabilitations/my own training), or my issues with familial breakdown, my inability to cope with past trauma or perhaps it is simply easier for me to blame social work as a whole profession? I can't honestly answer this yet, but I do hope one day to clearly know why I see the profession in dull tones.

One clarification I can give is that I believe, I feel, that social work failed myself and my brothers. Leaving us in a toxic neighbourhood, in a family that disliked us intensely (though our mother loved us immeasurably) and in an environment that has since caused me to openly use the words "care has saved my life, if not for care I believe I would be in prison or Dead." Even after deciding to home me, a decision not made lightly and made between me, the social work, and my mother on a voluntary basis, though at the time it felt like I was being dragged kicking and screaming. Even though it was decided I should leave, the social work still left my brothers in conditions of prevalent gang culture and poverty. As questioned above, perhaps it is simply easiest for me to blame social work, manifesting in my head this endless battle of right and wrong, of David and Goliath? A worker once said to me that newly qualified should abandon any hope of making structural change as the system would never allow it, paraphrased sentiment not a quote. I have tried to heed their advice, to move along and accept a quietened position of compliance, but whether I personally am to blame or social work is to blame for my upbringing, I cannot shake the sense that social work is an enemy that is looming over me and I must find a way to work alongside it for the better, I must find a way out of its shadow or be swallowed whole in what feels like an endless struggle, perhaps the only one I can remember clearly.

We must all strive for change and not be jaded by previous experience or negative rhetoric and going forward we must lean on each other for hope, support and reflections, good luck in your work alongside care experienced people and I hope you find them as enriching as I have.

Harrison, N. et al. (2020) Employment and further study outcomes for care-experienced graduates in the UK. Higher education. [Online] 1–22.

Reid, W. and Maclean, S. (Eds) (2021) OUTLANDERS: Hidden Narratives From Social Workers of Colour: From Black and Other Global Majority Communities. (Lichfield) Kirwin Maclean Associates.

REFLECTIONS

A page to fill

- Jo Thompson

I remember that Tuesday night at Youth Club. The theme of the activity was Who am I? My favourite youth leader was running the session and I usually fully embraced the many topics we covered. This one though, I wasn't so keen on. As everyone around me busily worked on their paper with words and drawings, I stared blankly at the page, taking more and more time over the heading I had written in bubble writing, with a delaying tactic of increasingly elaborate colouring in.

As the child of a father who grew up in a children's home and a mother raised in a convent, I knew little if anything of my heritage. My parents had experimented with some religions, but we were now placed firmly in no man's land in terms of beliefs. There were no baby photos, and no one talked about me as an infant. Who am I? As a 13-year-old I really had nothing to say. My favourite youth leader, astute and perceptive, lent over my shoulder and told me not to worry, and that I had a whole life to live and that he just knew I was going to fill that page right up!

What I did know was that social services were involved with our family after I was born. The story I had developed was that this was due to my mum having post-natal depression following the birth of me - her 6th child. It was never discussed. When questioned, my parents' response was a loud silence and heavy sighs. I have some vague memories of foster families (of varying quality and kindness), a lady with a nice dog who took us out on Sundays, and meetings at our house.

One day last year I received an email containing my files from children's services. I was shocked that my past just showed up in my inbox. I think I had expected to be forewarned, maybe offered a meeting? Isn't that how it works? Damn. I should know this stuff! I'm a social worker! I should know how this works! If this was an adoption file, I would have had a meeting, someone to sit with me and look at the files. Instead, I sat at my kitchen table, with these emails glaring back at me. Too much to send in one email – this is exciting and daunting in equal measure. I opened the files early one morning, close to Christmas, with my husband next to me. He is there, my anchor, holding me still as I enter this potential storm.

It's hard to say what was the biggest shock, my Mum's vehement rejection of me, the disdain directed towards my parents by professionals, or the lack of a child centred approach in this 1970's system. Astonishingly, in the whole file, there is actually very little about the children, practically nothing about my older siblings. It's really all just about my parents, and about professionals trying to manage these two very unwell people.

My older siblings have talked about some aspects of it, and they too were 'Received into care' a number of times. But they were children themselves, and their memories and perspectives were that of children. I know now that I have seen the information, they knew little of the reality of what was taking place.

As an adoption social worker, I know the importance of your story, your history and identity. So why had I left it until my forties to seek this information? Fear of what I might find out, upsetting my parents, my siblings......myself? I have never identified myself as a care experienced social worker. On panels, or training or anywhere. Why? Because I didn't know my story. I didn't know what to say had happened. I couldn't tell, because I didn't know.

I was eventually returned to my parents care on a permanent basis and there were no more social workers.....but there were still problems.....and with the knowledge I have now, I am intrigued by the decision that I was returned and left in the care of 2 adults with such profound mental health problems. I am surprised that for the duration of my childhood, my parents were left to parent me.....or I was left to parent them.

There have been many improvements in the way information is recorded, and I have some thoughts and suggestions from the experience of reading my files and also reading files of children I currently support.

I would urge social workers to write details about the child. We repeatedly document concerning incidents and themes on files and forms, and this is important. We also record in detail about what the parent did/said. The child will want to know about the situation in relation to them. Where were they when the concerning incident happened? What did they say and how were they afterwards? Describe what they were doing when you visited them at home, what toys they played with and if they interacted with their siblings. This is the kind of information they may never get from another source. Help them know what they were like and who they were.

Demonstrate curiosity in your recording, such as 'I wonder how the child felt when...' This shows that you were holding the child in mind, that they were important and that their wellbeing was the absolute driving reason for your involvement and actions. When reading my file, it very much felt like my parents were the clients, and not, in fact the children. A child's daily life is heavily documented once in foster care, let's give them more information about the time with their birth family.

I acknowledge the challenge in doing this when we need to so carefully record details of the concerns, and ensure we gather sufficient evidence. So many of the documents we use do not lend themselves to child centred recording. Approaches are used which are a step in the right direction for file recording, but there is room for further development.

Ultimately though, I am extremely grateful for those recordings, and for the laws that mean they were retained. Without this, a huge part of my identity would still be missing. Some of the file was so incredibly hard to read, and there are parts I wish I could unknow. But finally, I have my story. I can tell it – should I choose to. That means more to me than anything. I am aware of my challenges, there are aspects of life I find so hard, still today. However, now I know my early experiences. Understanding the impact of relational trauma, attachment, neglect, parental mental health issues and domestic violence, allows me to forgive myself for what I need help with, for the mistakes I have made and for the work I have to do every day. I have a great deal of empathy for that little girl.....for little me.

So next time I present an adoption training, or attend a workshop, I might just introduce myself as a social worker - and a care experienced person. I certainly bring that to my work every single day. I feel incredibly passionate about child centred recording in files. I feel great empathy for children with missing information and can truly appreciate the impact of this on their sense of who they are and who they will become. We must make sure that the young people we work with can know their story, develop their identity, and fill their page.

A Statement

- Narges Qauyumi

"Narges to think about what tasks she needs to focus on with the young person. The young person is keen to hear about her life history and doing activities such as attending temple has been positive, but Narges needs to focus on maintaining boundaries in the social work role. Next visit to focus on pathway plan and post-18 plans"

I would like to acknowledge that all personal details have been amended to preserve the identity of the young person referred to in this reflection.

The above is an extract from my last case supervision with my practice supervisor. To give some context this is a Looked After Young Person who entered care voluntarily. Jamie was transferred for me to case hold given the young person was settled and all court paperwork and procedures were complete. I was supporting this young person for 2 ½ months and during this period, I had visited her twice. In my second statutory visit I supported Jamie attend her place of worship. Jamie is a fiercely independent young woman who has a good sense of self and surprisingly strong values and beliefs around politics, race, and mental health. However, like most Children in Care Jamie struggles with making ends meet given the lack of financial support available to her. She lives in a rural area and wakes up 5am to get to college on time if the trains show up!

Jamie expressed that she wished to go to a Temple during my second statutory visit and I agreed to support her with this. The temple held late meditation sessions open to public members of the community. This was between 6-7pm. Their

Facebook page which was their only source of communication did not make this clear as everything was written in Jamie's native language which she cannot read or write.

Jamie asked on the day of our visit if we could stay longer and participate. Without going into great depth Jamie shared with me her familial experience as an adopted child and that of her culture and religion conflicting to that of her white upbringing. Jamie shared her experience with me which made me feel the time I chose to dedicate to her in that specific moment was invaluable. As a care experienced social worker who is in a capacity to take initiative and be the change that is needed in the system, I was pleased to be able to support her. I took great pride in sharing that safe space with her.

I have come to understand that in social work practice there are many processes and procedures to follow and if there isn't one specified then this is created, amended, and implemented. These processes can feel like an endless vicious cycle.

Reflecting on the extract from my case supervision, I felt like I was being told as Jamie's social worker to maintain my boundaries. I do not recall my supervisor writing this during our supervision. I accessed my case supervision notes simply to see what actions I was expected to deliver and complete. I was playing catch up with my timescales amending my online diary to reflect and prioritise my deadlines. When I read my supervisor's reflection, I felt confused, betrayed and in many ways retraumatised.

My state of confusion - I remember during our supervision session reflecting on how social work boundaries would reflect in practice. What this means to me as a care experienced social worker. I recall my supervisor asking me to reflect on this and what statutory duties I must comply with, I remember acknowledging and accepting these duties and attempting to make sense of how such processes guide practice. However, reading the extract from my case supervision and upon reflection I find myself asking; are my boundaries being questioned? Have I done something wrong? What is the role of a social worker and have I interpreted this correctly?

My feelings of betrayal - I saw this reflection weeks after our supervision, I do not feel this reflected my thoughts and feelings at that time nor does it reflect how I feel now. I do however feel this represents my supervisor's thoughts and feelings. Yet the way in which it is written does not clarify this clearly. Or am I reading too much into it? I felt we had a mutual understanding during our supervision on what I recall was a productive reflection. As an ASYE social worker in my first year of practice I am learning that my role is forever expanding as I familiarise myself with the policies and procedures and the complex integrating interactions between these. Equally, I am learning that I am expected to prioritise processes over real outcomes that stem from 1:1 interaction, this involves giving time to what matters to a young person prioritising them over a process that inevitably I am expected to follow. I am in a constant state of playing a balancing act; though reading articles from Community Care leads me to believe care experienced or not this is a shared experience amongst social workers in the profession. My question in this reflection to those reading is: How do we reclaim value based social work practice that is not so process driven?

Feeling retraumatised - I take great pride in the experiences I share with children in care. Our ability to collectively connect with our experiences of what it means to be in care; whilst also acknowledging the differences between our familial history and trauma allows for us to share a safe space that does not require any form of explanation. Many things can remain unspoken, yet we accept, and relational experience shared between us that feels phenomenal and surreal. This is my reason for becoming a social worker; why I entered mainstream fostering; why I cared for my sister as a Family and Friends Carer. I felt retraumatised reading the extract because I felt as though I was back in that same position where I felt disempowered. I was back in the position of a child in care being told I was wrong. I was again experiencing my words and actions being misinterpreted and misrepresented. Yet again I found myself in a position where it is my word against that of my superior. I felt shame that this was written in the young person's file; how would she interpret reading this on her file? Is this how she will remember me?

I find there is a different level of understanding that comes with bringing about change to the generation of children in care who are struggling with their identity. I have learnt that there is no right or wrong way of being, no one can bring value to your story and the emotions you experience from your trauma. No one can understand you better than yourself. I am who I am, you are who you are, and that is good enough. It has to be.

I value the insight that comes with being a care experienced social worker. Being in a position of power yet having had the experience of what felt like being disempowered as a former child in care; to me means my values, beliefs, and boundaries are not in conflict in the same manner as that to my non-care experienced social work colleagues. For instance, as social workers we often use the phrase corporate parents. What does this even mean?

Put simply, the term 'Corporate Parent' means the collective responsibility of the council, elected members, employees, and partner agencies, to provide the best possible care and safeguard to children under local authority care.

In line with care planning requirements as set out in Volumes 2 and 3 of The Children Act 1989 and the 2010 Regulations; local authorities need to reflect how to support children and young people develop their sense of identity to enable them make sense of their early life experiences, reasons for entering care and family relationships. Where appropriate

REFLECTIONS

this will include focussing on co-producing quality life story work with the young person. However, in instances such as Jamie's who has come into care towards the end of her teenage life and on the verge of becoming a young adult; many young people in similar circumstances as Jamie's *'fall through the net'* as their experience of service provision and delivery does not reflect to be equal to those children who enter the care system at a younger age. The question to be asked in this instance, whose responsibility is it then to provide and meet Jamie's needs?

For me, if a service provision does not exist to allow me to delegate and refer a young person to a specific service. Then. If it is to be, it's up to me as an individual worker to support the young person with that. Accountability starts and ends with me as a practitioner. Does it not?

I often find myself in positions where I interpret things in a literal form. Perhaps my brain is wired differently, perhaps how I make connections to form meaning and understanding of my surroundings based on my experiences of trauma highlights why I practice in the way that I do. I am not ashamed of that; I don't see myself as different and yet I often find others point out the difference in me and so I am made to feel different despite following the same legislative guidance to that of my non-care experienced social work colleagues. I know I have a radical rebellious edge to how I practice. I am an activist. I am a care-experienced social worker. And this leaves my social work self the question; How will I survive this?

We make the road by walking... the journey to becoming a qualified social worker

- Kyla

I graduated from university at the age of 40 with a first-class honour's degree, and award for the best dissertation and best overall performance within the school of health and social work. I spent from the age of 12 until 18 in the UK care system, and this is a whistle-stop tour of my journey to becoming a social worker.

I was born outside the UK and spent my early childhood moving around the world with my father's work, I can't remember the exact age I came to live in the UK, but I believe I was around 7. My home was not a happy one, and at age 12, the police turned up on my doorstep and arrested a family member. I was taken to a local children's home. I never returned home.

My time in local authority care was in the '90s, and I was mainly accommodated in children's homes. Due to various moves, my behaviour became harder to manage, and I would go missing. Subsequently, my placements would break down, resulting in multiple conversations about how I was 'jeopardising my future' and that I was 'on a one-way ticket to nowhere'. Furthermore, as I had already exhausted the children's homes in the town, I needed to be placed out of my local area. I would routinely hear professionals refer to me as a 'Hampshire Child' during these moves. Referring to me by my local authority may have started due to funding issues and going missing, but it had a profound impact on me growing up. I learnt that no one wanted me, and I attracted a 'budget'. I actively felt like a burden, a parcel, a problem, and a cost. When I was placed in one placement, a social work manager revealed the cost of keeping me there as if it was something I should be grateful for. Subsequently, when this placement broke down, I felt like I had let everyone down at great cost. I'm sure this was not the manager's intent, but this, combined with my care experience, led to me feeling a combination of hopelessness and shame. Consequently, once I had left my last residential unit at 18, I buried my care experience and learnt to blend in. I did not tell my husband's family, new friends, or employers of my care experience for fear that I may be judged, first as a person but, more importantly, as a mother. This fear of being exposed and therefore judged became even more powerful when one of my children had additional needs, and I was thrust into the world of assessments, professionals, and meetings.

Due to being in the care system and experiencing frequent moves, I left education at 14 and had no GCSEs. In addition, having moved so much, different exam boards made it impossible for new schools to issue me work, resulting in me spending the last years of my education colouring in. It was an unwritten assumption in the '90s that education was out of reach for individuals in children's homes.

At 18 when I left care, I was considered too old to get funding for GCSEs, yet I could access funding for A levels. Frustratingly, I could not access A-level funding as I had no GCSE'S, so I felt caught in a catch 22 situation and was unable to attain a traditional education. Due to the systematic barriers, I encountered, I discovered and enrolled on a Sociology course offered by the Open University (OU) and started to get an education. Fortunately, the OU had no entry criteria, and I was entitled to funding as I was claiming benefits. The OU opened many doors for me and having an identity as a 'student' rather than a 'care leaver' opened up many employment opportunities. I subsequently found my way into working in social care. I did exceedingly well in my early career and predominantly worked within hostels, housing, residential care, and youth justice settings. I never disclosed my care background. However, after having children and austerity policies decimating the supported housing sector in which I worked, I decided to pursue a career in social work. I saved up enough money to place my children in childcare to access the level 2 Maths and English qualifications I needed to improve my chances of getting a place at university. When I eventually applied to university, I did not tell anyone apart from my husband and friend Tracy, as I felt almost certain that I would not be offered a place at university. In addition, I was worried that I would be viewed as attempting the impossible and needed to be realistic in my aspirations. The possibility of attending university had never been pitched as attainable for me given my care trajectory and lack of qualifications; I felt like an imposter just completing the application process. However, Tracy was unwavering in her belief in me and gave me the strength and courage to try.

To my shock and surprise, I was offered an unconditional place at university to study social work, and I began to believe my dream could be possible. However, due to two part-time OU courses that I had completed at age19 and one awarded certificate, I was declined student finance for the first year. My hope of attending university was dashed, a night of devastation was followed by a week of several pleading phone calls to student finance that amounted to little more than a muttered 'sorry'. In order to study at university, I had to find the first year's tuition fees. Subsequently, the only option I was left with was to take out a personal loan. I will admit that having to take out a personal loan to cover fees is an area that I am still slightly bitter about as it meant I had to work solidly throughout the first two years of my degree. However, having access to university has given me life chances, which I otherwise would have never had the opportunity to access. On reflection, I feel very privileged to be where I am today. I firmly believe that there should be no limit on student finance for care experienced individuals. Care experienced students have faced multiple disadvantages and disruptions in their lives. Education has been the path to freedom and healing for many care experienced individuals, including myself.

Enrolling at university was a culture shock as it transpired that I had to declare whether I had any Social Services involvement in my life. That feeling of being judged differently and exposed flooded my life as if I was a child again. I worried that having declared my care-experienced background, I would be asked to leave; to me, it felt like a 'trap'. I filled out the forms and made myself 'small' as I was worried that bringing any attention to myself would fit into the narratives surrounding students and social workers with lived experience. Narratives such as 'it is too close to home', 'too much' and perhaps we need 'more work on ourselves' and the dreaded 'wounded healer'. Consequently, having submitted the required information and exposed my care 'status', I was further told that due to my age I was not eligible for any support; this was not done in a nurturing kind way, but a poorly worded email from student support asking me if I was an 'eligible care leaver'. The irony here was I was not looking for support, but had I been, this may well have led to feelings of rejection and abandonment. I wondered if it was because the university may get a 'premium' for attracting care experienced students and again it felt like a 'commodifying experience' rather than an authentic offer of support.

Furthermore, despite my older age and therefore ineligibility of support, it was mandatory to fill out any involvement with Social Services. When I have later challenged this, I have been most often told it is to highlight that 'support' may be needed. Frustratingly 'lived experience of social services' is placed among criminal convictions and disciplinary procedures in Social Work England admission guidance; making it appear that lived experience is viewed as a potential risk. Paradoxically, work experience in Social Care is looked upon as an asset – the disparity is palpable and fits very much with the stigma of how I fear care experienced professionals and social work students are viewed within the profession.

Overall, the degree was a testing time for me. I was exposed to entrenched views about children's homes, children in residential care, and care experienced parents. At times, I had to seek external support to help me navigate my responses and keep my emotional reactions in check. However, three lecturers were a beacon of support. With these lecturers, I found I could actively challenge views about policy, stigma, and explore what changes need to occur at a national level to improve outcomes for care experienced young people. Despite my lack of basic education and missing huge periods of school, I excelled academically and socially at university, becoming the unofficial rep, support person, and advocate for many students who I am lucky enough to now call friends.

In addition, I was fortunate enough to have entered higher education when it was being recognised that care experience is lifelong and never leaves you. Consequently, I was invited to be part of a group for care experienced students and lecturers in higher education. Within this group of individuals, I finally found a 'home', a feeling of not being different, out of place or an afterthought. This group of wonderful individuals have inspired me to continue my university education, and I am now undertaking a part-time masters alongside frontline practice. Having this affinity with a group of care experienced students and lecturers really highlighted the benefit of finding shared heritage and its impact on the feeling of belonging.

Within my university experience, my practice placements were the most prominent and impactful part of my learning journey. In my first practice placement, I was placed on a child in care team. Subsequently, I was apprehensive that I would hear the stigma that has been so persistent through my life, attached to the children and young people I would be working alongside. However, I couldn't have been more wrong. The team was outstanding and really championed the children and young people they worked with, often going above and beyond their duties to improve the life chances of the young people in their care. Within the team my practice educator Kate was particularly perceptive and noticed my knowledge of language and became curious. Kate brought her intuition into supervision and stated she had worked with several care experienced social workers, giving me a hook to disclose if I felt comfortable. Being able to be honest about my heritage, worries and how I may be perceived was the antidote I needed to continue with my degree with confidence that my care experience would not hold me back. The safety net of having a practice educator who would embrace my questions, reflect on my worries, and build my confidence was life-affirming and highlights that relationship-based practice is not just limited to working with families, it is just as life-changing when working with peers and students too. In addition, Kate and the team highlighted to me that perhaps I was able to work in statutory services and that my care experience would be an asset in building up my ability to manage the job and deal with the uncertainty it can leave you with, rather than something to be hidden and swept under the carpet. I never really got to thank the team or share my experience with them directly due to the pandemic. But I did ensure that the assistant team manger was aware of how impressed I was by the practice and support I was able to witness.

For my second practice placement I was placed in a frontline community hospital discharge team with my practice educator Sadia in the middle of a pandemic. Walking into a team mid pandemic really highlighted to me the emotional toll and trauma that practitioners were having to face. Sadia was the only social worker within the team, and we were one of the only teams in the area conducting home visits. Experiencing the pandemic in a front-line team, whilst dealing with families who were clinically vulnerable was one of the most overwhelming experiences I have had in my working life. Nothing I had learnt at university or in life prepared me for witnessing the fear, trauma and thankfulness of the families I was privileged to work with. Subsequently, every practitioner in the team became really close and the solidarity is something that I will never forget. Within this placement I chose not to share my care experience with Sadia as I wanted to ensure that my focus remained on what I could do to support the team. In further reflection, I think there was also a desire to test the belief that Kate had in my practice. There are many narratives that are often attached to individuals with care experience such as survivor/hero, victims or as liabilities/risks. I wanted to be sure that my practice was judged on unbiased evidence that was undistorted by my past or stereotypical entrenched binary views of 'who care experienced people are' and 'what they are like'. My practice placement was again positive and in addition Sadia turned out to be one of the most humble practice educators I know, and we have since become firm friends.

Whilst working within adults was an amazing experience, my passion was still with children and families. Therefore, I decided to develop my practice and start my assessed and supported year (ASYE) in a children's long-term safeguarding team. I interviewed for a few positions and although asked in the interviews 'why social work? I never felt able or safe enough to refer to my care experience as being a reason why I have chosen to enter the profession. I think this was due to a combination of not wanting to be labelled as 'different' but also because that question then automatically leads to a natural curiosity as to what circumstances led to me being taken into care. Being open about my care experience has never been an easy decision as it opens a 'Pandora's box' and lays my whole childhood open to scrutiny. I think we have a tendency to naturally assume that people have lived a similar life to ourselves, similar values, we can imagine different housing, even different cultures to an extent. But anything that sits outside of our normative views tends to spark curiosity. Subsequently, this natural curiosity can then mean that I am left feeling vulnerable, defensive and worried about the questions that may be asked. Consequently, being open about my heritage is not a simple as it first appears.

I was lucky enough to secure an ASYE position in a protective, nurturing, and good local authority. I have not shared my care experience with my line manager, but I have informed my ASYE practice consultant that I am care experienced. This revelation did not come in the early days of our relationship but came about as a natural progression of reflective supervision. Importantly, I have never felt that my practice consultant has looked down on me or questioned my ability to practice given my prior experience which again has been refreshing and allowed me to be honest in my reflections. I am not opposed to sharing my care experience with my manager, but it would need to come up as a natural part of conversation rather than me feeling I need to reveal or tell something about myself. Feeling cornered to disclose my care experience, like at university, feels too much like the power dynamics of being a child and every professional knowing your story. Consequently, after having so many details of my life and everyday care recorded, handed over, or spoken about, anonymity has an almost serene quality for me at times.

One of my biggest fears entering social work in a local authority near to where I was accommodated was that I would meet practitioners that worked with me as a child. I think this had also made me a little wary of what local authorities felt safe enough to work in. In my current local authority, there is a worker who crossed paths with me as a child in an unqualified capacity. We both have tried to unpick if we actually were in the same place at the same time and are unsure if we were, but she knows my care siblings, previous social workers, children's homes and managers. My initial fears about being outed are now much less, it was actually nice to feel validated and be able to have a shared history and sense of belonging, something that is incredibly rare when you are estranged from your family and your history is fragmented due to systems, processes and professionals.

I have not made a habit of telling other social workers in my local authority about my care experience as I am not sure it's needed or relevant. I do, however, get quizzical looks and questions when it appears I have good knowledge and understanding of diverse topics despite being new to the profession. My age and prior work experience affords me a privilege that I can hide behind, something I am acutely aware that younger care experienced social workers may not have. This offers me that easy get out of jail free card if I want to back away or find a loophole to escape from questioning. I do ponder at times if this reinforces the view that care experience is something to be ashamed of, as I doubt I would have the same concerns about revealing I had lived abroad or in a boat or something that would still spark curiosity. This ambivalence is something I have learnt to sit with over the years, but still question myself about frequently.

Retrospectively, whilst declaring my care experience at university was traumatic and exposing for me, it has led me to see that I do not need to feel ashamed of my care heritage. Consequently, in being more open about my care history I have found and been welcomed into a community of care experienced social workers and professionals. Being part of a care experienced community has meant I have found a diverse group of practitioners with whom I can share my reflections, frustrations, and worries. Significantly, within this supportive group, it has become apparent that several care experienced professionals who have been honest about their care heritage have felt this has been used to discredit their voice and beliefs whilst at university and within employment. My primary commitment within my role is to the families that I am privileged to work with, and if sharing my care experience with colleagues could disadvantage my work, it is a risk I am unwilling to take. Therefore, I do not see myself as an ambassador for care experienced social workers or an activist for change in this arena. In addition, talking about my care heritage opens difficult conversations as to why I was in care and what that looked like. Children's homes are stigmatised and viewed very differently from other forms of care, and the children are labelled more so. I have already faced the perceptions around children's homes and the children that require them at university, and I'm not sure I'm ready to fight that battle as a new entrant to the profession just yet.

Sadly, undertaking this degree and my entry to children's social work has had a personal cost; some biological family members have been unhappy with my career choice, I have experienced lots of negativity, and projected hurt that has meant that my journey into the profession has been profoundly lonely and has involved loss. This has meant at times I have questioned if the 'cost' has been worth it. However, when I have seen the changes within families and witnessed the power of making individuals feel seen and heard, I know I have made the right choice.

I was once labelled as 'Traumatised', 'Risky', 'Maladaptive', 'Hard to place' and even 'institutionalised.' I hope that the lens you choose to look through with some of the young people you walk alongside is not one that attempts to predict their future or categorise them and further trap them in a box. I am not my adverse childhood experiences, my trauma, or my care experience alone. My past does not predict my future. I am not in need of pity, pedestals or to be an inspiration. My name is Kyla, I like chickens, travel, reading and the sea, I have three wonderful children, a handful of lovely friends and I am a social worker who happens to have been taken into care as a child and this was a whistle-stop tour of my journey into social work and some of the barriers I have encountered along the way.

My journey and thoughts, as a care experienced newly qualified social worker

- Hannah Ide

When given the opportunity to share my narrative as a care experienced social worker for this book, it was hard to know where to begin, or how much I should say. As a child, I felt silenced and as though my voice was unimportant. The adults around me dictated my life; I had no choice or control in where I lived or who I built meaningful relationships with. I went into the care system aged ten, following my mother becoming sectioned due to poor mental health. From a social work perspective, you could say I had faced many adverse childhood experiences: abuse, neglect, domestic violence, mental health problems, lone parenthood, and substance misuse. As theory and research may support, these experiences meant I found it difficult to form relationships with foster carers and I moved placements over twenty times, within eighteen months and this was following short lived stays with various family members. I suffered severely from anxiety and obsessive-compulsive disorder, for which I saw CAMHS and was given medication, but I could not seem to settle in foster care. I did not understand why I was not allowed to be at home with my mum and younger brother. Aged twelve, after exhausting all foster placements I was moved to a children's home twenty miles away from my school, where I lived for five years until I was seventeen years old. The adverse childhood experiences continued within the children's home. Our needs were complex, and the staff lacked skill or training to be able support the mental wellbeing and welfare of the children within the home. I won't go into the details, but those five years were some of the most traumatic of my life.

At seventeen years old, my mental ill-health had become quite severe, yet I was still forced to moved out of the children's home and live on my own in a flat. Although living in the children's home seemed to make my mental health worse, living alone when I did not feel ready was not the solution. At this point, I had not long started my A levels at college, this move made me feel unsettled and effected my ability to complete assignments and exams. Moreover, at the start of my second year when I turned eighteen all support from social services and any financial help was ceased. This meant I could no longer afford to get the train to college and was asked to withdraw due to low attendance. During this time, I felt lost and was without a fixed abode, I had no money and could not provide myself the stability I desired. I rented rooms from strangers, lived in a foyer, stayed in flat shares...it was like being in care again, constantly on the move. I tried to live with family to give myself the opportunity to save money and go to college, to get a career... but this broke down within a week. By the age of twenty I was homeless and unhappy living in a B&B and then a hostel. I wanted to leave my job in retail and do something more meaningful, but every avenue I pursued seemed to have obstacles.

Whilst living in the hostel, I spent some time at the local library to explore my options. Although I knew I didn't have the grades or money for university, I still browsed the courses and pondered what I'd like to do and what I'd be good at. My work experience consisted of retail only, however at age twenty I had more life experience than most people of old age. I wanted to use these experiences for good and to help others, I knew my rare insight could contribute to something meaningful. After much thought, I decided to apply for social work, not only would this provide me with a stable job which I desired more than anything, but it is a career that I already know so much about from my lived experiences. I applied through UCAS and managed to get an interview. However, the journey from here was far from easy... nonetheless, one year later I started a social work degree at a University previously rated best in the country. I was so happy to be out of homelessness and to be starting this new chapter of my life.

I was eager to learn more about the role of a social worker and how I could best help others who were vulnerable within society, like I had once been. However, as I progressed on the course, I started to feel that perhaps I didn't fit in with the ideal image of a social worker, and that my care experience meant I wasn't good enough to fulfil such a role, contrary to my prior beliefs. Admittedly, I was perhaps not entirely ready at this point in my life to become a social worker, but as a care leaver time was not a gift I was given. I had chosen to share my care leaver status with my peers and lecturers, as I thought this would be a positive thing to do, however I soon learned that sadly there is a discrimination and stigma attached to having this care leaver status, sometimes subconscious, sometimes fully intended. I decided at this point to withdraw from the course, as I did not feel I had the support I needed, and I was not sure if I would ever return. Two years went by, during which I spent some time working in a residential home for adults with learning disabilities. A fire then re sparked deep down within me and I felt ready and more determined than ever to become a social worker. I spoke to the original university I had applied to, nearby where I lived, and they agreed to let me join on the social work programme from the second year. I remained motivated and managed to graduate with first class honours this year. Although this university journey was six years altogether, I am grateful for this because only now do I feel I am truly prepared and ready to be a social worker.

At University the second time round, as time went on and it felt relevant, I did share some of my experiences as a former looked after child in classes, however, most of the time I remained quiet due to a fear of negative labelling or a stigma being attached to me. I knew I would not receive any more funding from student finance and that this was my only chance to become a social worker and provide myself with a stable future. I know from my social media presence, that many other care leavers within the profession have shared similar anxieties, following negative experiences where they have felt discriminated against. My beliefs were that if I remained quiet and was agreeable, I could get by and complete the course. In a profession that promotes equality and social justice, I initially did not understand why I had been treated the way I had by those who supposedly believe in such values. However, I soon learned that we are all humans, forever growing, developing, and making mistakes. But this is why I wanted to contribute to this book because it is a step in the right direction, a step to acknowledging the true worth of care experienced social workers. I have shared some of my journey, with the hope it will raise an awareness of how much knowledge and understanding these lived experiences can give.

Care experienced social workers have endured so many of the adverse experiences troubling children and families today, and we have come through the other side. Many professionals understand how our lived experiences can positively influence and contribute to good and effective practice. However, sometimes I've been made to feel like I shouldn't share this part of my life. I don't want to hide this part of my life, nor should I have to. But sometimes it is not about choice, sometimes this part of my life and the trauma I've faced comes to surface whether I want it to or not. I recently got diagnosed with a chronic illness, that has many symptoms but predominately for me the main issues are extreme fatigue and sensitivity to pain. Much research suggests that chronic illness can happen following long-term stress and trauma, the connection between being care experienced and having chronic illness is undeniable. This health condition, alongside having anxiety, OCD, body dysmorphia...many may think, how can I be a social worker? The trauma has literally rewired my brain, I don't think like everyone else... However, I've learned the importance of reflection, to understand my feelings and I use this to support my practice and decision making. I'm not perfect, but I'm doing the best I can to better myself, develop my professional identity and use my lived experienced for good. I now do share my care experience with fellow professionals, and my disability, because I believe I cannot be the best social worker I can, if I'm not my authentic and true self.

To conclude, I believe as the social model supports, with the right support, adaptations, and changes within my working environment, I can thrive despite my lived experiences, disability, and mental health issues. The same principles of empowerment and strength- based practice that we use to support those we work with, should also be used to support care experienced social workers. We are RESILIENT, EMPATHETIC and DETERMINED individuals with so much to offer the social work profession, but the social work profession needs to recognise our worth, recognise the positive contributions we can make and support us through the tough times. I'm thankful this book is being made, because I think it will help those within the profession to appreciate how valuable care experienced social workers are, and I'm looking forward to reading the narratives of others. Sometimes, it can feel very "us" and "them", "professionals" and "service users", like there is a divide, but care experienced social workers bat for both teams. We can feel torn, forced to dismiss our care roots in our professional capacity, or feel like traitors to those we grew up with in care, for joining a profession which previously represented so much bad, so much heartache and pain in our lives. But I'm proud to be care experienced, and I'm proud to be a social worker, and these should never be mutually exclusive. Working for a local authority who used to be my corporate parent is a strange feeling, but with support and the right adaptations I know I can be an asset to the profession, alongside all the other care experienced social workers. I'm proud of how far we've all come, and I'm proud of where we are all going!

REFLECTIONS

Learning to live with it

- Victoria J

I was aged 25, when a glossy pamphlet on adult learning was lodged through my letterbox. Herein the prospect of *real study* was ignited by chance. I am of the ilk, to try anything once, so I sign up to a course in my local library. My learning thereafter takes on a steady pace. I am still naively unawares as to how this will serve any end goal. Nor do I understand the social mobility, status or position education can create for one in society.

I am however, content with gaining another certificate to add to my ring binder (gained through work based training) I was undertaking shifts in a residential home for young people in care at the time.

School wasn't pleasant for me growing up because many of my peers knew about my situation from quite early on. My English teacher announced this to the class *'in our midst we have a pupil living independently in their own flat!'* He thought this a novelty. I had turned 16 in the October, after having broken down a foster placement, moved to my own accommodation. It was the late 90's, so void of any aftercare services. But this teacher made a celebratory gesture to the class because I had simply attended for the day. Many assumed Looked After children simply didn't bother to show up and I was the anomaly. This new found notoriety and kudos amongst fellow pupils was a pleasant feeling at first but mostly I would use it to counteract how inwardly alienated I felt. I craved stability and didn't like being a rare entity amongst a group of spotty teenagers. Soon after I took a downward spiral and I started to live up to their expectations. This was an affluent school I attended which made the contrast of my situation sharp and stifling.

A sinister turn of events happens from here on in as living on my own in a flat meant I was a sitting target for every reprobate in the local area. No questions were ever asked when I arrived to school in expensive convertibles or would be missing for several says at a time. Who could the school actually report this to? I was responsible for myself or so I thought. Studying social work was tough when covering topics on CSE, CCE because this was a phenomenon I was well versed to, except there was no labels or theories to describe this at the time. I would like to pause on this bit and fast forward to where I get enrolled at university...........

As a care experienced person, I subscribed to the notion I must work harder to be more credible, that someone would soon come along and suss me out as an imposter, when in reality, I was actually doing quite well. I had found my calling, as cheesy as it sounds. I was piecing together my own past and using this as muse. Albeit the emotional challenges came from learning topics that were sometimes jarring and close to the bone, here is where I first learnt to compartmentalise as a professional. Nonetheless, social working others invoked a sense of in me that I started to thrive off. I felt compelled to do good work, always. I very quickly earnt the respect of my tutors, then much later my work colleagues.

I often chuckle now when I think of the way I would contribute in class using third party scenarios to describe my own life. I stuck my hand up during a lecture on professional boundaries......... *'I knew this pupil at school who entered care having been physically assaulted at home but there was no placements so she went to stay with the teachers'.*

I was three years into the degree when I eventually admitted this person was me. This was the first major milestone of self-discovery, the point when I openly shed a protective layer to others and it felt safe. I spent a long time using the course in this way to test out how it felt speaking out loud whilst being in search of the acceptance of others.

I suppose it's important to note the near misses too, such as my first-year placement in a hostel for adults addicted to substances. My own father was using heroin at the time, having done so for most of my life, so it was a world with meaning attached to it, yet emotionally, I was unravelling. This is how my course tutors came to know about my personal background.

The idea of social work became very conflicting for me, I became the rescuer of hopeless endeavours, spending excess time offering talking therapies to the tenants, asking one to write their feelings about their estranged child down in a letter. This was too much for the chap and it led to a spike in his drug use. Taking on reflective practice, I now know by getting the drug user to acknowledge his child, was meeting my need and not his.

However, crucial lessons were learnt and I become accustomed with Prochaska and DiClemente's cycle of change. I then returned to university after this placement with an even hungrier appetite for anything theory. My tutors commended this transition in me and graduation went ahead.

Learning to live with it in professional circles

I began my ASYE with a typical rookie mentality. I had basked in reaching what I thought was the finish line. I look back with some of my ex-colleagues and we laugh and remember the time I tried to suggest (to a desk full of seasoned workers) *have you lot thought about using this theory when considering your interventions?*

The first manager I had, came across as quite jovial at first, he wore a suit and tie and commanded a presence that fell a little short of his actual competence in practice. Witnessing his approach with families was awful, he was quite abhorrent in his tone and manner with little awareness of the use of power. I started to become quite subservient in this dynamic nonetheless. After a few weeks I fell off his radar and relished in the autonomy to find my way as a newly qualified.

I undertook my first assessment and travelled out of area to consult with a family member to discuss, with the mother's consent, her support networks. I returned back to the office and was greeted by said manager who took me aside to question my whereabouts. He was angry for not getting his expressed permission on the home visit. He told me he would let me know end of the day if I still had my job.

By 5pm, I had shadowed a strategy meeting, sick to my stomach and white around the edges. What followed has become etched in my mental archives and I have used this example, many times when explaining the use of power and control in practice. I sat in the room with the principal manager who was very confused as to my reaction, she had not been privy to my ordeal of being told my job was at risk, instead she reiterated the importance of keeping the whiteboard up to date, so here I learnt about the lone working policy, which is perfectly acceptable looking back. What was not acceptable, was that a misdemeanour such as this was used to pull me in to line, bully and threaten me unbeknown to his senior. I left this meeting sobbing and desperate to keep my job, stupidly believing this to have been a sack- able offence.

I explained that I had experienced being in care and that this was my life's work and purpose, and I would have expressed this in the interview but I had held back. This is no exaggeration, his response was...... if we had known this you would not have got the job.

I shut down after this. I did not enjoy my work as I felt constantly under suspicion. I exhausted myself going the extra mile at every opportunity to prove myself, all the while the misconception of social work dawned on me and shattered my hopes and dreams.

Fresh hope and getting in touch with Jad

Jad or Dr Jadwiga Leigh, as she is now known, is someone I consider to be on Parr with the late Mrs Hope and Mrs Ellis, teachers who pulled together and put me up temporarily when I entered care. Jad was someone who genuinely cared about what I had to say. Even though I never knew her as a social worker, she was definitely a social worker I would want to have. Jad was my lecturer at uni, she introduced me to Erving Goffman, Canadian born writer who talks about stigma and shame. Goffman argues that stigma relates to the notion of 'devaluation', in which an individual is disqualified from full social acceptance. I used this in a presentation exam and scored high. Jad went onto to become Chief Exec to a pioneering project helping women to parent their children again. Still feel blessed to have her in my contact list.

After leaving uni, Jad got in touch to enrol me on a project she was researching that involved a load of practitioners, clay and the People's history museum. This work gave me the chance to offload about the organisation I worked for in a way that was unparalleled to any case supervision. Here was borne the sculpture of the uplifting hands, an artefact I produced that was featured on display in the museum, the front cover of PSW magazine, complimented by Harry Ferguson and displayed at the care experienced conference.

This definitely wet my appetite for other projects and since then I have produced a short story entitled 'No frills foster care', a talk at the Care experienced conference and made my way up to where I am now as a Team manager of a busy fostering team.

No Frills products was a known supermarket range. My foster carer would purchase these and place them in a separate cupboard to the rest of the household.

I use my experiences to help social workers construct meaning and perspective for children in foster placements. I became empowered to leave poor cultures in social work behind and I have contributed to learning by producing a podcast for students during the pandemic which teaches them to consider the nuances when entering a home for the first time with child welfare concerns.

I am now proud to say my personal experience of the care system binds me to social work in a unique way and I feel I have healthier roots in the profession than I once did. This is a thanks to the professionals and organisations that are inclusive to all, that give colleagues room to grow and space to those learning to live with it in professional circles.

REFLECTIONS

Am I flying (yet)?

- Mary Carter

"The moment you doubt whether you can fly, you cease forever to be able to do it." (**'Peter Pan' JM Barrie**)

It's been quite a week. On Friday I was back in touch with my Psychiatrist, Dr V who I haven't seen since I was a "LAC" teenager; he was as shocked to see me as I was to see him. So much had changed in eight years and I was a "new Mary", well at least that's what I wanted him to see. I was surprised that he was still around. For as long as I can remember, I have trained my mind into believing that being strong means you have to be ok all the time. It was my duty to stay ok, I don't want anyone to worry, and I don't want anyone to pity me. So, since as long as I can remember I close that bottle up and toss it in the sea. This worked pretty well until I qualified as a social worker and self-reflection and self-awareness became part of my everyday thinking and doing. This version of me was never going to last, it was inevitable. As social workers, we like to show that we have it all together and we can handle anything that life throws at us, professionally and personally. I think even more so for us care experienced practitioners. Shame makes us desperate to prove to everybody that we can do it and we can achieve. A lot of people will tell you that you don't owe anyone anything other than yourself, advice I have had a countless number of times. Easier said than done though, right? For us, it's almost an instinct. It's not just a desire that arises all of a sudden, but rather a deep-seated need that has a very long history.

Today I start on Dr V's recommendation this week, writing things down. "Why should I write it all down?" I asked as he handed me a pen and pointed to my 6 clear notepads that I had planned to journal in but left in a pile collecting dust. I chose not to point out that I was the national Student Social Worker of the year in 2019 and that I had not long graduated from Anglia Ruskin University with a First-class honour's degree in social work. I wasn't being dismissive, I genuinely wanted to know how it would benefit me. He gave a small sigh, as if the answer was blatantly obvious. He remembered how hard I find it to talk. At that moment, I had a strong sense of relief - he remembers me. Most care experienced adults will know the feeling of having to repeat your story, your journey and your experiences over and over again. I just kept saying sorry, I don't know why and what for, sorry for being wobbly, sorry for being back or sorry for wasting his time. Many people have told me over the years to stop over apologising, this has always been my default, a habit I have struggled to unlearn. Keeping the emotional waves calm, wanting to do anything to avoid the pain of someone potentially being angry with me.

Education and learning has always been my safe haven, my escape and my blanket; school, college, university. Despite some horrific childhood experiences and deep internal sadness and pain throughout this time, I referred these to Dr V as the only three places I have ever really felt safe, physically and emotionally. I worked hard, I achieved well; higher than the average "beat the odds" as they say when a young person having been in the care system does well. My tendency was to distract myself with my studies as a way of coping and defending against my pain, the pain I was so adamant I had already worked through. I have always been driven and conscientious, pushing myself too hard at times. I always felt I was never doing enough, I had to do better. I just could not settle and remain still even with the accolades I was awarded. Social work became part of my identity, I finally thought I had got to a place where I developed a positive sense of who I am. Identity has been one of my biggest battles throughout my adult years, who am I, what am I and where do I belong? On reflection, when I started as a newly qualified social worker, to myself I feel I identified as a care leaver first and a social worker second. I've had to really work on this and my thinking as it was holding me back. That was my past, I am Mary Carter, I am a social worker who happens to have care experience.

I've been on the receiving end of social work, and I've seen the way in which young people's voices are ignored. Their feelings and wishes are recorded, but very little changes. Every child has a deep-rooted wish to have better relationships with their social workers. I've been on the providing end, seeing the impact and damaging effect of a "broken system" on a child's life yet seeing little outrage about this within the workplace. And I've felt utter sadness for children, the sense at times I feel as "corporate parent" as part of the problem, re-traumatising them by providing them with incompetent services that are meant to be in place to help them heal. Feelings of frustration with how professionals present as emotionally disconnected. On the face of it, being able to overlook what's going on. Social work was my calling, an opportunity to change things. I felt having direct experience of the care system meant I could and would bring something different to the profession, more insight, more curiosity and more passion. I had an endless reserve of positive energy to give.

I was successful in my social work interview, and I was excited to join a social work team at a time when a new generation of passionate, committed and driven social workers was very much needed. It unquestionably felt strange starting a new role during lockdown, where I didn't have a full team around me for help and support. Alongside this, the narratives I had created in my mind anticipating how people would behave towards me or treat me if and once they found out I was care experienced. Would they judge? Would they feel sorry for me? Would it go against me when my judgments and decision making is explored? or would it change the dynamics in the relationships I had with my colleagues? Why do I have such a fear? It's my identity, one I should be proud of. I mean let's face it if I can't own my story and be proud of where I am how can I expect the young people I'm supporting to do so?

I was warmly welcomed and by connecting on our teams WhatsApp and remotely via Microsoft teams I began to feel comfortable asking questions, seeking guidance and opportunities for learning. I became part of a team that wanted me to grow and a team that saw potential in me. For the first time in my life "stability" felt real to its word, and I was exactly where I needed to be, doing just what I should be doing. I felt at home, a feeling I craved to have for as long as I can remember. Research evidently shows how relationships are the golden thread for our young people, the start to their healing. It was the start to mine. Some of the people and colleagues I have made connections with since my social work journey began have made a huge impact on my life.

One of my university lecturers, now a very special friend, once posed the question: if I asked you to name all of the things that make you happy and give you fulfilment, how many other things would you be able to say apart from work? This hit home, this question served as a reminder that many of us live to work. For me work was and always has been a distraction, the only thing I felt I had full control over in my life. It gave me purpose; it gave me hope.

Admittedly, it's nice when your talents, attributes and abilities are recognised, when your work is rewarded. In these moments I feel my existence is justified. I feel flattered, I feel important, and life feels good. Yet I continue on this perpetual mission to prove my worth and to satisfy others. I change and mould myself to fit in and ultimately, I exhaust myself striving for endless external goals, while neglecting my own spiritual and personal growth. The expectations I felt were upon me, I was putting on myself.

I'm sure many of you can relate in some ways to my experience; the feelings of judgment, of difference, and the need to please everyone around you in order to feel accepted. The 'I do not need anyone; I'll get through it by myself' conditioning has been my survival tactic for many years. To shield myself from betrayal, disappointment, abandonment from those who would not and could not be there for me. If I don't ever put myself in a situation where I rely on someone, I won't be disappointed when they drop the ball, as they will eventually drop the ball right??? Never again I promised. I ask social workers to think about this in relation to the people they are supporting.

Becoming a social worker encouraged me to look deeper into myself, and what I am now able to recognise is that no matter how much I have dressed it up and displayed it proudly to make it seem like this level of independence is what I always wanted, in truth it was my hurt, sad, confused and lost self behind a protective brick wall. This desperation to please others over any care to myself was my response to trauma held in my body. I told myself that I am only safe when other people are pleased with me. I learnt to funnel my understanding of myself through the imagined eyes of other people and it was exhausting. I may have felt a relief when I met someone else's standard of approval, but it was only brief, more typically, I was left with a nagging sense of emptiness. How I felt in the inside, is complete contrast of how extremely put together I appeared to everyone from the outside.

While writing this I continue on a journey of a self-discovery, one I appreciate is never ending. We all have fears, mine is the fear of abandonment, except I never really knew this. I never really understood how by being there for everyone else but not caring for me, I was in turn in acting my own fear. This learning has in some ways been comforting. I sometimes need to let people down to honour my own needs, I have had to disconnect with people to reconnect with myself and that's ok. Healing will take time, I have a lot to unlearn and so much more to understand but as Gabour Mate (2008) so wonderfully says, "the beauty of healing is that when you re-frame it and see the source within yourself, you become powerful". This will continue to be a process that involves hard work but every day I can stand tall and reflect upon my awareness that is growing. My past may have moulded and shaped me, and my brain may be wired in a different way to others, but it does not change me as a person and the values I stand for.

As I have touched on, in 2019 I was honoured to win the most prestigious award of Student Social Worker of the year, still my proudest and most memorable moment to date. I remember for days after this event feeling like I was a celebrity, the press pushing me to send articles, a number of radio stations inviting me to speak. I was overwhelmed with joy and shock. It was a strange feeling, a care leaver looked after by the state winning such an award. How did this happen? There were thousands of students all over the country who deserved this just as much as I did.

As wonderful as it was, soon after an article with the captivating heading "student social worker and care leaver overcomes adversity to win gold award" was shared far and wide. This reinforced the feelings of shame I so often experience all over again. Why the adversity? Why the care leaver - is this relevant? I still question this to this day. Would that grab more attention from the public? Would that be more interesting? I also felt fearful. Very few people knew that I was care experienced, in fact only one person in my cohort at university was aware, now the whole wide world was to know, will I still remain safe, does this mean Mary number 1, 2, 3, 4 and 5 will be identified? How will this sit with people? Will they be shocked? The lid I screwed on my past is going to be opened, my stomach churned. Sharing my care status was something I have always felt very uneasy about, my story and my journey was a subject I never spoke about. My prayer was that this would be old news quickly and there would be something much more interesting to talk about. My lecturers knew I was care experienced and they were incredibly supportive and accepting and displayed pure kindness, they saw me for me and continued to be my cheerleaders. I thank my university for the opportunities

I endured, the connections I gained and the confidence I built.

As incredible as winning the award was, I did struggle to manage the praise bestowed upon me as a newly qualified social worker and I felt the expectations on me to do well were extremely high. Truth is, I created these expectations myself. To gain my colleagues and managers approval I became the "yes girl." I shied away from who I really was, my own uniqueness. Again, I created this myself. In my mind this was all too good to be true. This feeling couldn't possibly last. I was waiting for that moment when someone taps me on the shoulder telling me "They have caught me out". Imposter syndrome at its very finest. How long will fighting against the negative stereotypes that care experienced people face last and how long can I avoid the self-fulfilling prophecy of failure before it becomes a physical reality? I was certain that this dream was soon to be over.

I was chuffed when I saw the news that a care experienced group was to be made, one where social workers from all over the country, from different disciplines could find a safe space to share their experience, insight and support. An area that is very much needed. I, for one, know that so many of us share similar joys and upsets, yet sometimes these remain hidden. Personally, this group has given me a sense of belonging, hope and reinforced determination. I am looking forward to seeing what we can produce, how we can support social work education, develop professional practice through research and how we can continue to ensure that we remain the brightest beacon of light to our children, the children that are our future, the children that professionals must not give up on.

What seemed to stick with me the most from just two meetings as a group was language. This appeared to be a very important matter for us all. I wasn't surprised to hear that every one of us had experienced a situation where the poor use of language was expressed, whether this was from conversations with colleagues, in supervision with a team manager or within a professionals meeting. The language of care unfairly labels children, and professionals are often complicit to it. We subject our children to language and processes which are unhelpful and hard to understand. This is often done without intention but without thought of impact or consequence. The jargon and negative connotations used makes our already traumatised children feel different, stigmatised and in my view, this contributes to many poor outcomes across the board. Although movement is happening, as we know change is slow. I ask all readers to be mindful of their dialogue. Such words can have a detrimental impact on children and their livelihoods. A challenge for me has been adapting the way that I work to try and help young people understand that what we are trying to do as professionals is help them and work with their best interest at heart rather than against them. This was something I found difficult to accept throughout my time in care.

One of the hardest things I have had to understand as a social worker is in the wake of trauma, although I desperately want to, I cannot take away the pain for these children. We all want to do this on some levels, we are social creatures subject to emotion and when we are around people that are hurting, we hurt too. I think my own personal experience gave me even more desire and fire to do this. In truth, it is not that simple. We can however help children to begin to heal.

The struggles I have endured are what allowed me to identify and care about pain in others. The external validation I longed for (and continue to long for) I see other children and care experienced adults feel just as deeply. Stories and journeys are different, but the emotional pain is the same, because all pain is the same. I wouldn't be who I am without the trauma. I have learnt how important perspective is, when I shifted my mindset, I started to trust that everything that happens to us also happens for us. Compassion, kindness and warmth are all part of what moves me forward in every judgment and decisions and I will continue to ensure that my though process and thinking in social work remains as "it is not what is wrong with you, it is what's happened to you". I wonder is this something you do?

I would like to end with a message to EVERY professional that works with care experienced young people....no child should feel like they are not good enough, worthy or useless. Remind them of their self-worth, be consistent, be reliable, and be a practitioner that brings professional love back to life. It's easy for people to read stories about what happens to a select few in care but unfortunately, it's not a story, it's real life. Children just want to be understood. Children don't want you to feel sorry for them, but they do want you to understand that your judgments of them can be so wrong.

Mate, G. (2008) *In the realm of hungry ghosts: Close encounters with addiction.* Random House Digital.

I've Looked at Care from Both Sides Now

- Dr Trevor Rodgers-Gray

Despite being open of my care heritage today, that I am a care leaver, writing this has been much harder than I thought it would be. Not so much procrastination, more the raw emotion of recalling my biography. Stigma and shame are also present despite my rational knowledge to the contrary. I also ask myself, who would want to read this? Will it seem self-pitying or just boring, will it help or interest anyone? Is it therapeutic for me or might it be for others? In the end it is just one version of my story nothing more or less; if I type these words on a different day, whilst the facts would remain the same the story may be wholly different. It is the story of my experience in care, my life as a social worker and subsequently a social work lecturer, and the duality this entails. To borrow some words from Joni Mitchell, 'I've looked at [care] from both sides now', although if I am honest, and to use Joni Mitchell's exact words, 'I really don't know life at all'. I do like clouds though.

My first six years were immensely happy ones. My mother was a single parent who worked as a child minder. I recall how my mum would ask my brother and I to hide from time to time, so that it would appear that there were fewer children being cared for. They were brilliant times: a gaggle of children playing for the longest of hours. We were poor back then with no car or family holidays, and mum had no qualifications, no one in our family had gone to university, but then this was true for everyone else living around us.

My mum was diagnosed with breast cancer when I was about six years old. This was my first introduction to the world of social work: meals-on-wheels, home help, and a trip to

Alton Towers were some of the highlights – I enjoyed sharing the pudding delivered with the (usually) still warm meals. I remember fondly, my arms aching carrying the bags of shopping home the ½ mile from the local store, emptying out the commode, and cooking waffles and burgers or fishfingers under the grille for tea for me, my brother, and my mum. I was a young carer, not that I would have recognised this label at the time, nor did anyone offer support. Despite everything, this too was a happy time.

After my mum's death I was placed with my first foster family. I shall not dwell long, for suffice to say, they were abusive. They would provide only small amounts of food, such that I was always hungry (I quickly began shop lifting to supplement my diet, mostly chocolate; I became quite adept at this crime). They were violent. I still hold the frozen photographs of time in my mind of the fist coming toward me (the anticipation of it was terrifying). But worst was the control they held over me; it is difficult to describe even now: every aspect of my life was made not private and free from my agency. Now I was in care I was entitled to pocket money and a monthly clothing allowance, however I never received this, it was taken by my foster parents supposedly so it could be saved for me. There were occasional social worker visits, but I was never allowed to see them alone; I was too scared to ask, and the social workers never suggested this. You might wonder how it could be that a social worker would not see the empty fear in my eyes, would not ever ask to speak to me alone – I have no answer to that question only some context, it was a different time (years before the 1989 Children Act) so perhaps for some it was just normal practice. For me normal practice meant that it wasn't too long before I started drinking alcohol, smoking, and using drugs. It was at this time of my life, whilst still a child, that I was first arrested. It is a scary thing to be put in the back of police car, taken to the station, to have your fingerprints taken and your photo. That first wait in a cell (clearly with the intention to 'scare me' on to the right path) was the most frightening, although despite this I remember being fascinated with an adjacent cell with lurid pink walls; I was told it was to hold people who were 'psychotic' as it supposedly calmed them (I was and remain unconvinced of the veracity of this).

The loss of my mum I could make sense of, at least rationally if not ever emotionally, bereavement is of course a lifelong phenomenon. What hit me like a freight train was the loss of my two dogs (they were adopted I hope and presume, when I was put in care, or perhaps they were 'put down'). Of course, Freud would argue that this grief was compounded by transference, from the loss of my mum. Nonetheless, the lack of recognition by social workers and other professionals around me of the impact of the loss of my pets on me, in retrospect is disappointing. (I now know that such experiences were hidden, antecedent drivers silently, yet inevitably, pulling me towards the social work profession.)

Eventually I ran away from my foster home, and not too long after, made a telephone call to social services (I remember the smell and tight 'space' of the red telephone box distinctly). I was then placed in a children's home. It felt relatively safe, and I made a temporary new friend (another child from a 'failed' foster placement) and then subsequently lost contact with her when she was moved on. It is like that in care, at least my experience was, friendships and connections are transient, and belonging is an alien concept; my foster placements and residential care were in different towns and none in the town where I lived with my mum. One advantage of not belonging is that you are not so tied to tribal sensibilities – I have no football team or sense of ownership over any one place, and this for me feels freeing and provides a less parochial perspective. Whilst in residential care, I was involved in fights and got into trouble for starting a fire in my room; yet still it was so much better. Weeks later, I was moved to another foster family. The contrast from the 'evil' foster parents could not have been starker. The first evening we had a West Indian curry dish and talked, and I was listened to.

They taught me to cook, responsibility, but most importantly showed love and encouragement. We discussed politics and racism. It was good.

I stayed there until shortly after my 18th birthday when I went off to university (a care-leaver, not that I heard or would have recognised that label at that time). Just before I left a social worker came round with a glass tankard to celebrate my 18th. It was from the 'evil' foster parents. I was horrified; it was like being teleported into that abused child again. The glass slipped from my hands and smashed on the floor. It was at this point that I realised that nothing had been done, that other children might even be placed with these abusive foster parents. The sense of guilt mixed with horror was unimaginable. When I spoke to social services, I was told that no new children had been placed with them and that the 'evil' foster carers had chosen to stop fostering. Social Services said they would be removed from the register. I was asked whether I would like to speak to the police. No. Not just then. It was time to a new chapter of my life.

University was a roller-coaster ride adventure. For the first time, I felt I had complete agency over my life, and I threw myself into university life in all its extremes: particularly alcohol and drugs, and the poll tax protests. That first Christmas at the end of my first semester of university was strange. I had presumed I would return to my former foster parents for the break, but soon learned I would have to pay rent to stay with them over Christmas, and so I choose my only option based on my finances and remained in my own hall lodgings; my care from the local authority had ended. For me though, education was an escape. Somehow and despite exceptionally little work, I managed to graduate. I chose to read biochemistry as I had a vague notion of being a forensic crime scene investigator (long before CSI was a staple on our screens). I had briefly considered social work but dismissed it as too 'raw' because of my own care experience.

I went on to gain a MSc and then PhD in environment science (there is some evidence that academic achievement is a coping mechanism for children who are, or adults who were, abused and suffered trauma). Working, researching, and caring about the environment is an ethically based vocation. My work influenced EU policy (reducing the acceptable concentration of non-ionic surfactants in aquatic systems and advocating for reduced animal testing of hazardous chemicals); things I remain proud of. However, the silent pull towards social work had been gaining momentum and what felt as inevitable, even unavoidable, to live an authentic life became the decision to study social work. Of course, we spin our own narratives, and in so doing, assume there is just one clear path...the hubris of auto-biographic reflection.

My intention was to practice with adults: end of life care or learning disabilities. This was due to the internal barrier I had constructed that I could not practice with children and young people – I am not entirely sure why, perhaps for fear of triggering emotions? Or maybe I had already internalised narratives that care experienced people should not work as social workers with children and young people. Perhaps, more accurately for fear of getting it wrong – knowing as I did how high the stakes are for children and young people in care. I know now that that view was not formed from me alone, but also shaped by the views, myths, and stories of social work that flowed around my formative social work education and practice. And so, my first statutory practice was with the adult learning disability team. It was not long however before I knew I was being drawn to work with children and young people. The care management approach that was dominant at the time made the transition that much easier, as although many of my colleagues were fantastic, care management was an anathema. My practice with adults however did help me really see people as people, and to recognise the structural oppression that impacts on people's lives (I had been taught about Anti-Oppressive Practice, but it did not come truly alive, for me, until I was qualified).

REFLECTIONS

During my social work master's degree, I confided to my tutors about my care heritage. Whilst they were attentive and supportive, the emphasis was very much on whether I was 'ready' for social work and practice placements. The notion that I may have some lived expertise was never considered. I was guided to take my second, statutory placement with adults because of my care-experience; and I was willingly complicit with this decision. Later, whilst working for the adult learning disability team I never revealed my care heritage.

It was at this same time that I had my first child (now two). Interestingly, there may be a parallel between the social worker working with children who is / is not a parent / guardian themselves, and the social worker working with children who is / is not care experienced.

I finally came full circle, when I started working as a social worker for Barnardo's children service; here I really felt that I was making a difference. It was also the first time I really appreciated the duality of my experience: I was me the 'care leaver' and me the 'children's social worker'. This duality was an odd thing to live with. At the same time, I felt I was an imposter who lacked the skills and ability to be objective, and yet I also believed I had insight from my own care heritage: to take time to get to know the young people, really listen to and be with them, and to be able to share some of myself, my story. It was not all good times though. I disclosed to a colleague (though not my manager) that I was care experienced and I was told that I should not be practising social work because I have been in care. I somehow became a service manager, and a few years after that got my first social work lecturing post at the University of Plymouth.

Today, I am fortunate and privileged to work at the University of Bradford where I can not only be open about my care heritage but am supported – I work alongside our student care leaver ambassador and the faculty equality, diversity, and inclusion team where care experience is recognised as an important aspect of identity. I am open about my care heritage to the students I teach, in the hope that in some small way I am removing the stigma ascribed to being in care.

As a social work academic I am conscious that little is known about the challenges and insights of the care experienced social worker – this is an active area of my research. I also have a supporting role within the Association of Care Experienced Social Care Workers (ACESCW). Being a member of the ACESCW has given me a sense of belonging and has been a powerfully emotional experience. I have met some lovely social work students and practitioners. If you are a social work student or practitioner and have lived experience of care, then as a group we would love to hear from you. If you are interested in research in this area, you may contact me through the association, email, on Twitter or via the University of Bradford.

Multiple identities – carving out space for the personal, professional and the political within social work

- Rebekah Pierre

I have never met a one-dimensional social worker. Each of us carries multiple identities which shift and change according to what is required of us within any given moment.

By lunchtime, most of us have already worn through several of them – we may have acted as a sister, a social worker, a caregiver, or a friend, allowing the different (but often interwoven) qualities we possess to come to the fore as and when they are needed.

But within certain social work circles, there is a pervasive ideology around who and what social workers should be whilst at work – a sort of contagious fear about 'crossing boundaries' which leads to the assumption that the personal and professional should, under no circumstances, bleed into one another.

I first encountered this position in the first week of my role as a newly qualified social worker. Long before the days of virtual meetings, I was sat in a horse-shoe table set up amongst my peers, listening attentively to the trainer at the front of the room.

'Between 9-5, you keep your personal life at home. Keep it out of the office, and out of people's homes. You don't want to cross *professional boundaries*' she said, pausing before the final two words for emphasis.

'But what if' I asked tentatively, raising my real (not digital) hand 'there is a situation where sharing something personal might be really useful. You know, if all other interventions have failed, or in an exceptional circumstance or something'.

'Well', she said with a sort of renewed energy, 'you can always refer to your own story in third person to show that get where they are coming from'.

Uncertain or not as to whether she was joking, I half-smiled, before realising that she was in fact being entirely serious.

I never did use that technique; I think it was well-meaning, but it would have felt disingenuous to pass off my deeply personal story as someone else's.

Though I did take on board her clear message - that the personal and the professional were mutually exclusive. And so, gradually, I began to decompartmentalise my life, cutting off the care experienced part. It wasn't so difficult - I had already faced stigma around my care experience in university. The small amount of courage I had left about disclosing it had been well and truly extinguished by this latest exchange.

From this point on, I kept my care experience, with all its pain and sorrow, but also insight, discernment and understanding, hidden away. It would be years before I would dust this off and share it with the social work community.

In many ways, I can understand the need to guard our personal lives. For the people we work with to feel validated and heard, it is integral that we do not defer to our own experiences, compare situations, or disrupt a disclosure to make something about us. No, that simply would not do. There is also the argument that our personal experiences could be 'used against us' (although I feel this is rooted in fear and judgement more than anything else).

But there is no denying whilst social work is not about us, it does involve us. We are not just robotic agents of the state, walking around with our lanyards, to-do lists, and right-brained rationality. We also have hearts and memories, which could, under unique circumstances where careful planning and supervision are involved, be equally as useful in making meaningful connections. For how can we expect so much vulnerability from those we work with if we ourselves are so closed-off? And more importantly, how can employers expect their workers to fragment their own lives in ways which do not mirror reality?

I look back on certain exchanges with looked after children I worked with and feel pangs of regret. When Casey (not her real name), a terrified 15-year-old girl who had gone to A&E after a mental health crisis told me how overwhelmed she was, would it have been helpful to stand in solidarity and to say that I too had been in her shoes? And that my existence as a care-experienced social worker was a testament of hope?

Or when 16-year-old Nathan (also not his name) told me I could never understand what it felt like to rest my head in a strange place with people I did not know or trust, would it have helped if I told him that in fact, I did? And to share coping mechanisms or perspectives from my own life?

Or when multi-agency professionals dismissed me at a first glance on account of the intersectionalities of my gender, age or regional accent as they so often did, could I have mentioned that I was astutely aware of how the system worked, having lived through it?

Could I have gently said that in fact, I was an expert by experience, and perhaps I had something to teach them?

Of course, these hypothetical scenarios have no answer. I will never know.

But what I do know is this – this year, my perspective shifted drastically. I learned that as care experienced social workers, our collective lived experiences not only bring value, but they also have a rightful space within social work. We should take up much more space than we do.

Readers may be aware of the ongoing review into children's social care in England. At the time of writing, it is currently underway, having been promised in the 2019 Conservative general election manifesto. It aims to 'radically reform the system, improving the lives of England's most vulnerable children so they experience the benefits of a stable, loving home' (Department for Education 2021a).

As has been widely discussed elsewhere, whilst the review itself has been largely welcomed across the sector, concerns have been raised around the 'manner in which the Review has been announced, its framing, and how preliminary stages have been conducted' (BASW, 2021a). This coincided with recent ban on unregulated placements for children under 16 (Department for Education 2021b). Whilst this move worked to protect those 15 and under from unregulated placements, shameful policy announcement...[entrenched] a two-tier care system' (Article 39, 2021), by denying children under 18 the right to the same level of care they could otherwise expect in foster care or regulated residential homes'.

As the year wore on, becoming increasingly frustrated by policies which excluded older children from care, I wrote a paper entitled 'Revisiting Diary Entries from Care: An Exposition of the Challenges of Unregulated Placement Settings', which was published in Practice: Social Work in Action. It was an autoethnographic work in which I photographed extracts from a childhood diary I kept in care, specifically at the age of 16/17 and whilst living in an unregulated placement.

Anyone who has ever kept a diary will relate to me when I say that I was deeply self-conscious about anyone having sight of them. I only aired these because I felt it absolutely to expose the brutal reality of what life was like within these placements, in the hope of raising some awareness. I could not find any literature which centralised the voice of children in such placements and wanted to change this, whilst hopefully encouraging others to share their stories.

REFLECTIONS

The extracts contained what felt like fragments of my heart and soul – words which were witness to suicidal thoughts, self-harm, trauma and heartache. Before submitting the work, I wrestled with the ethical dilemmas, including that I could not time travel and gain consent from the child I was when writing the entries (Pierre, 2021). However, I eventually came to the conclusion that although my childhood self would have intensely disliked the idea of the diary entries being published, she would have agreed if there was a small chance of raising awareness about the physical, mental and emotional harm such placements can have on vulnerable children under the age of 18 (ibid).

When it came to publication, I wondered if I had gone too far – whether or not I had shared the unshareable. I felt quite vulnerable, as if someone (myself!) had ripped out my internal organs and laid them out on a table for the whole world to see. I woke up in the middle of the night wondering if people would view me differently, whether I would scare off future employers, or whether I had done the right thing in leaving an eternal digital footprint of my time in care.

But, like so many other times in my life, I was wrong – so wrong. Instead of being shamed or misunderstood, I was met with kindness and understanding. One social worker said they had never heard of an unregulated placement before reading it, which make me realise this; if we speak up and change one person's understanding, what we have been though was not for nothing. It can be put to good use.

And if we speak out, we can prevent others from swooping to the rescue to try to capture our voice or speak on our behalf. As a community, we are resourceful beyond measure. I have said this before, and I will say it again; 2 years in care taught me more about the system than any university course ever did or could. I have not only read about the impact of punitive policies, poverty, trauma or loss, but every cell and fibre of my being have lived through them. My five senses and I understand these issues from the inside out.

We need not decompartmentalise ourselves; we are not only care experienced, in the same way that we are not only social workers. Rather, we are capable of being both in all their fullness, able to integrate the two and to exist as who we truly are.

But we can only go so far without support. It is one thing to embrace our intersectionalities to their fullest by ourselves or within the care experienced community, but if we have no way to safely and meaningfully share who we are within the workplace, we will continue to have no choice but to hold back. With this in mind, below are some recommendations as to how employers and organisations can support care experienced individuals to thrive. These should be read in conjunction with the views of diverse care experienced social workers.

- Allow people to discreetly share that they are care experienced should they wish to. Given this is not a protected characteristic at the time of writing, many social workers 'go under the radar' and are not able to disclose this core part of who they are.

- Avoid harmful practises such as assuming we are more or less capable than others to bond with a certain family due to our experiences. Treat us in the same way you would treat any social worker.

- Ask if we may need any additional support in any area of work, but do not assume.

- Find an opportunity to work with us to map out our strengths and skills.

- Be mindful that festivals, holidays or religious celebrations of all cultures may be difficult or triggering.

- Invite us to mentor or teach those in senior positions about our lives (should this be something we are willing to do).

But do not rely on us to do the work or educate others – encourage others to learn more about care from a range of sources and voices.

- Be mindful in group or personal supervisions when asking others to share about their family lives or their past – take the lead from the care experienced person as to what their limits may be.

- As with any employee, learn about the unique intersectionalities we may bring (should be willing to share them), and engage with us in a way which is anti-discriminatory and anti-oppressive. Burnham's social GRRRAAACCEEESSS model (2012) and the LUUUTT model (Pearce and Pearce 1990) are tools which can be used to engender discussions around intersectionality within social work teams.

- If there are opportunities for us to contribute to innovation, invite us to lead and design these alongside care experienced children, rather than being drafted in in a tokenistic way. Train us to research, manage projects, audit, or whatever skill is necessary – we are capable of all and any role. Co-production is about equal partnership, not about finding space in pre-planned work.

Article 39 (2021) "Education Secretary gives green light to two-tier care system." Accessed 16 March 2021. https://article39.org.uk/2021/02/19/education-secretary-gives-green-light-to-two-tier-care-system/ [Google Scholar]

British Association of Social Workers (2021a) "BASW England policy statement on the Independent review of children's social care." Accessed 16 March 2021. https://www.basw.co.uk/media/news/2021/feb/basw-england-policy-statement-independent-review-children%E2%80%99s-social-care [Google Scholar]

Department for Education (2021a) "Education Secretary launches review of children's social care." Accessed 16 March 2021. Education Secretary launches review of children's social care - GOV.UK (www.gov.uk) [Google Scholar]

Department for Education (2021b) Unregulated accommodation banned for vulnerable children under 16. Accessed 16 March 2021. https://www.gov.uk/government/news/unregulated-accommodation-banned-for-vulnerable-children-under-16 [Google Scholar]

Partridge, K. (2019) PSDP Resources and Tools: Social GGRRAAACCEEESSS and the LUUUTT model. Accessed 11 November 2021. https://practice-supervisors.rip.org.uk/wp-content/uploads/2019/11/Social-GGRRAAACCEEESSS-and-the-LUUUTT-model.pdf

Pierre, R. (2021) Revisiting Diary Entries from Care: An Exposition of the Challenges of Unregulated Placement Settings, Practice, DOI: 10.1080/09503153.2021.1979503

REFLECTIONS

Shame, Social Work, and Transformation

- Richard Devine

When my dad was 8 years old, police officers and social workers rushed into his home and he *'immediately ran under the cubby hole in absolute terror'*. I can imagine a little boy, tucked away and hidden in a dark corner, pulse racing, adrenaline saturating his body, eyes wide, hearing highly sensitive to any impending danger. Suddenly, a hand reached in to grab hold of him. Out of fear and panic, he resorted to animalistic self-protection and bit the person. He was eventually dragged out from underneath the cubby hole. He and his brother and sisters were photographed by the police before being separated and placed into care.

Before this episode, my dad's mum had already left the family home to begin a new relationship. This constituted the first amongst many forms of abandonment my dad was to experience throughout his life, although I suspect that this was the most profound. After his mother left, my dad and his brothers and sisters were cared for by his dad, who abused his sister. This was discovered by professionals unbeknownst to him, and without any forewarning, he was removed.

27 schools later, multiple different care homes, including one in which he was sexually abused at knife-point, he went into adulthood traumatised, angry, fearful, impulsive, and addicted to drugs and alcohol. He met my mum when they were both 17. My mum was the youngest of 7, the only one of her siblings that went to Grammar School, but naive and seemingly drawn towards helping the un-helpable.

At the time and age that I write this (aged 34), he and my mum had 4 children together. His adulthood so far had been characterised by instability, ongoing drug and alcohol use and episodes in a psychiatric unit due to drug-induced psychosis. During this time, my dad was dangerous, violent, unpredictable, and impervious to my mum's desire and attempts to help him. My mum remained infatuated with him despite his flaws, desperately and unyieldingly clinging onto his potential – a spark she noticed that showed he was and wanted to be more than a violent drug addict defined by his traumatic experiences. She would also occasionally glimpse the love that he had for her, and the power of this would encourage her to persevere with the relationship. This took its toll, and, in the process, she needed to block out the psychological pain invoked by his harmful behaviour, but her body kept the score (to borrow from the title of Van Der Kolk's 2005 book on trauma).

By the time I was born, change had occurred. My dad wrote proudly in his diary, '*I attended the birth and held my wife's hand, and he was born, and with some sobriety he was the only child born while I wasn't actively addicted*'.

Several years passed, he attended university, became a social worker, and achieved the greatest level of stability and contentment in his adult life. Perhaps my mum's unnerving belief in him had paid off – she wasn't misguided after all.

Unfortunately, it didn't last. My dad left his job on health grounds, finding it hard coping with long hours as well as my mum's deteriorating health. The years of living with my father compromised her immune system, physiology and her body was giving in - she developed hepatitis C and nearly died. Once this passed, severe depression and chronic fatigue set in.

To make matters worse, as soon as my dad stopped working, he began drugs and alcohol using again. He wrote in his diary, '*it was shortly after I left my job, I took one pill and within a short period of time I was a fully-fledged alkie and druggie, my son Richard saw some of the old behaviour that he had never experienced before, and I feel this contaminated him...this disgusts me*'.

When this happened, I was 8 years old. He was right, I did see some of the old behaviour. It was a childhood of two halves.

One memory from the first half of my childhood involved me and dad in the front garden of our council house on a warm, sunny day. He was stood adjacent to me, took hold of my wrists and I held his. He began spinning around until enough momentum was achieved and my feet lifted of the floor and I was soaring through the air. The combination of risk invoked from feeling as though I was flying yet being firmly held by my dad created a sense of felt safety and immersive joy.

Another memory from the second half, occurred during a family holiday. My dad was clearly intoxicated on alcohol, benzodiazepines, and heroin. He was driving me, my brother and sister down a winding and at times, narrow coastal road at dangerously high speed. My sister said, 'Dad can you slow down, you are scaring us'. He slowed down suddenly and proceeded to drive at a painfully slow pace as traffic quickly accumulated behind us. 'Dad, I didn't mean for you to drive this slow' and he picked up the frightening speed once again in a childish retaliation to my sister's request. Whilst this was occurring, I turned to look at my brother sat beside me. I observed him close his eyes tight shut, place his hands over his ears and lean forward. Completely shut down. Avoid sensory input of the danger and ignore all internal signals that this was frightening. A good strategy I thought to myself, and I copied, ameliorating although not removing the unbearable fear.

During his relapse, my dad had left me - where had he had gone? He was still there physically, but on a more fundamental level, he increasingly disappeared, relationally and psychologically. I was devastated. I felt deeply sad for my loss, yet unable to do anything about it so began shutting off emotionally. My mum began disappearing too - she slept more and sank into depression.

To deal with the rejection and utilise what limited availability they had to attend to me, I dampened down my dependency needs and suppressed and hid feelings of sadness or anger, having learned my parents were not able to deal with or respond to such feelings. A rule I established was 'don't express feelings'. Furthermore, I sought to please and placate my unwell mum because when I did this, I elicited a more favourable reaction. I established a second rule, 'constantly think about and anticipate my mum's needs'. These two rules combined led to the development of a largely unconscious strategy of (1) minimising my own needs and (2) anticipating and meeting the needs of others. It was effective, given the context I found myself in, however, it accompanied a pervasive sense of inadequacy and worthlessness that derived from having my emotions unintentionally yet persistently ignored or devalued by my mum and dad. My child self could not separate the rejection of my feelings from rejection of my fundamental self. Shame was the outcome. This was what we shared in our family, shame.

Shame because my dad was rejected by everyone who should have cared for him

Shame because his drug and alcohol use hurt those around him

Shame because my mum couldn't protect and shield her children from violence and drug abuse

Shame because she couldn't be the parent she knew she could and wanted to be

Shame because when my dad turned to drugs, I thought he didn't love me

Shame because my mum's depression left me feeling rejected and unlovable

Shame...

At 16 years old, one week shy of my 17th birthday my dad died. The doctors said he died of cancer. I think he died of trauma and shame. To me, psychologically at least, my dad died 1000 times before he physically died. Every time I approached him or sought comfort or attention from aged 8 until 16, and he was unavailable or rejecting, our relationship suffered a blow, as did my sense of self.

At his funeral, I didn't cry. My best friend attended, and he cried. 'How unusual' I thought to myself as I peered over my shoulder and observed him wipe the tears trickling down his cheeks. I had spent the last several years detaching myself from emotions – especially negative ones. I had become so efficient and effective at this I didn't even know I was doing it.

After he died, I asked my mum, '*why did dad become a social worker?*' She replied that he had told her it was, '*because he wanted to prevent what happened to him happening to others*'. I was saddened on his behalf that he was unable to fulfil this ambition, and probably because I was overly attentive to his needs, wishes and desires, I decided in that moment that I would finish what he was unable to.

It wasn't until several years later, however, that I learned what my dad was attempting to achieve. At a social work conference I attended, a psychotherapist explained that many of us in the helping profession often attempt to rescue our childhood selves vicariously through helping others. Suddenly, what my mum had told me about my dad's reasoning for becoming a social worker several years prior had new meaning. My dad was attempting to rescue his childhood self. It also occurred to me, that I was attempting to rescue my dads' childhood self on his behalf.

I carried the feelings of shame and a sense of inadequacy into adulthood, throughout my social work journey. This was quite a powerful motivator – a desperate desire to help others and a fear of never being good enough propelled me to relentlessly improve. I was unable to acquire a sense of self through who *I am*, therefore derived it from work. Although it was a punishing way to exist, it produced some positive real-world effects (a good job, decent salary, etc). It seemed to me that everything good in my adult life was borne out from pursuing social work with these underpinning motivations.

However, this was an unsustainable approach. I presupposed that I could rescue my dad's, or even my childhood self vicariously through helping others, which I subsequently realised was well intentioned but, ultimately, futile. Secondly, I was desperately seeking recognition and validation to compensate for a deep-rooted inner dissatisfaction, yet whatever positivity I received externally only transiently ameliorated this internal anguish, which remained largely unaffected. Shame weaponised my ego into becoming a punitive, tyrannical judge constantly criticising me, and harshly reminding me of my worthlessness, especially if life circumstances provided some evidence to the contrary.

I was conflicted. I needed to get rid of what was detrimental, but it is hard to let go when the shame helped me achieve my goals of becoming and being a social worker, and all the positive consequences that came with this. I needed to find a way to transform otherwise the motivation derived from shame, irrespective of how well I progressed, would keep me feeling worthless. I would remain deeply unhappy, suffering quietly and perhaps, eventually resign and self-sabotage, like my dad.

I had remained connected to my dad, despite his death, through continuing his unfulfilled ambition and our experiences of shame; our shame had different sources, but it was an intergenerational, and somewhat comforting, bind.

I subsequently accessed therapy through an organisation called Concorde. The strategy that I developed helped tremendously in childhood and created some benefits in adulthood but left me bereft of any meaningful connection to myself and hindered my relationships to others. Through the work available Concorde, I began to cultivate a new awareness and appreciation for my internal experience. I became aware of how often I would bend myself to be liked, or avoid disapproval; how much I avoided emotional intimacy because my experiences had associated intimacy with pain and rejection; how I would be willing to lie and be dishonest in an attempt to avoid potentially upsetting someone (and thus experience rejection), or undermine the carefully calculated and crafted representation I had sought to create; AND how much of my attempt to avoid my sadness only left me disconnected and depressed. For the first time, I was able to process what was hitherto suppressed, mainly sadness. Paradoxically I felt tremendously gratefully to being able to experience the sadness. Being able to tolerate and process negative emotions, also gave space and opportunity to experience lighter, positive emotions. I was able to realise that my desire to help others and motivation to improve didn't necessarily need to be sourced by shame, and in fact, I could access a greater power in the absence of its prohibiting and suffocating constraints.

I think that overcoming the shame that I inhabited also has had a transformational effect for my dad, albeit in spirit, and now allows the more positive aspect of who he was, and the influences that he had on me to flourish. His potentiality is expressed through me – this is how we are connected now. It has taken me most of my adult life to realise that death can have a redemptive dimension, but it required a painful process of introspection to access this in respect of the loss of my dad. In simple, yet profoundly poetic terms, Eckart Tolle (2003, p.108), a spiritual teacher writes:

'**Death is not the opposite of life. Life has no opposite. The opposite of death is birth. Life is eternal**'.

The Trouble With Me

- Elizabeth Tusting

It has taken me months to sit down and write this piece, and as I begin to type, I know that there will be a good reason for my reticence and not just because of work commitments. Initially I had been thinking about my experiences as a care leaver working for many years in children's social care and I had considered that the nature of the work attracts people with certain characteristics and life experiences and therefore it is reasonable to assume that feelings of self-doubt and a fragile confidence are not exclusive to being a care experienced person working as a social worker. I am also mindful that I have been a social worker for longer than the duration of my childhood, and I am curious about whether over the years my identity has evolved as a social worker and less so as being care experienced. For the majority of my career, I have never shared that I was once a looked after child, I reflect upon whether this has been a protective mechanism and remember the clear message I was given when I first embarked upon my career in social work at the tender age of 19 years

I was in and out of 'care' most of my childhood and then at the age of 11 years I was made subject to a full care order. As I type this, I deliberate my use of the word 'subject' and realise the relevance, because in those days being 'subjected' to care proceedings was by far the least child-friendly process and to this day, remains possibly the worst day of my life. This was before the Children Act, around 1982 and as was the common practice, my sisters and I were required to sit in the court room and listen and observe whilst our mother made incredibly distressing statements about how she no longer wanted us, did not care about us, never wanted to see us again and demanded that we were 'taken away'. It was ferocious and a terribly cruel process in a system that was supposed to care for children.

I was the oldest of our sibling group of five and had taken on the parenting role of my sisters whilst we lived with our mother and so the social workers, in their wisdom had made decisions (obviously without consulting or speaking to us) that we needed to not only be separated but kept apart to allow my sisters to 'settle' in to their new placement, therefore we had not seen each other since we were removed over a year earlier and we missed each other terribly. In my immaturity I made a joke to my sisters and we all began to laugh loudly, we were ordered (by the judge) out of the courtroom, followed by our foster parents who were angry with me for disrupting proceedings and misbehaving. I did not understand then (nor seemingly did anyone else) that unconsciously in distracting us, I had tried to protect us; I just felt the burning fire of shame and guilt for what I had done. As if the day could get any worse, as my mother came out of the court room and left the building I tried desperately to follow her, calling after her, I was restrained by social workers as I desperately tried to free myself to run after her, when finally I did, she was long gone. Our foster carers looked at me with horror and disgust and I was reprimanded for causing my sisters further distress, my actions were later cited as being the reason why I was not allowed to have contact with my sisters, because I was 'trouble', I have caused trouble, and reinforcing what I already knew, that I was bad!

Many years later one of the social workers present that day in court, told me it had been the worst day in her working life, her statement validated the pain I had experienced, in a way that I could never have allowed myself to appreciate on my own.

I was placed with a foster carer who was an alcoholic, the family dynamic was dysfunctional and my foster carer was abusive towards me, physically and mentally and neglectful including withholding food and locking me away in an extended part of the house, adjacent and separate to the main home which was little more than a building site, unfinished with breeze blocks, no plaster, concrete floors and no heating, I did not even have access to a toilet and was passed one plate of spam sandwiches daily from the main door of their home - to this day I hate spam! I spent most of my time outside of the foster home, stealing food and begging for money, selling anything I could find or even steal from shops (the familiar shame rising as I type) so that I could buy clothes from jumble sales, one Christmas I was able to knock on doors singing carols and pretended I was collecting money for a local residential home for the elderly, I managed to buy myself a new pair of jeans. I spent that Christmas in the kitchen with the foster family's eight large dogs (Airedales), I was allowed out of the 'extension' because the foster carer's parents were visiting and so I was given egg and chips for Christmas dinner, I recall telling myself that the meal should have been called 'dog hairs and chips' as there were so many in the meal.

My social worker never visited and then after I ran away and rode 16 miles from one town to another, to look for someone who knew my Mum, I was picked up and returned to the placement where my social worker was waiting to move me, I had only seen him once prior and from there I was taken to a children's home. I didn't really understand why I was moved, except that I was told I was 'getting into trouble' or my foster carer thought I was 'too much trouble'.

I was moved to a very strict children's home managed by two exceptionally old-fashioned elderly women (known as 'aunts') who were cold, judgmental and rigid in their ideas about how children and young people should behave and present, (seen and not heard). I missed my mum and sisters terribly and I had no idea where they were, I absconded a lot – mostly to find my mum or my sisters, and to escape the overbearing aunts, I used to spend my time in phone boxes, trawling through the phone books looking for names that my mum might be using or of people associated with her.

One day she visited me for the first time in the home and during her visit, we arranged that I would I abscond again, and she collected me and I went to live with her in another part of the country, this was not agreed by the local authority. I lived with my mum for about a year before I contacted the local authority myself asking to return to their care as living with my mum was not working out, and all I really want to write about that time is that my physical and emotional wellbeing deteriorated significantly through living with my mum. As I sat on a wall, waiting for a social worker to collect me, I decided I would 'keep my head down, finish my time in care and turn my life around'. I was returned to a different children's home where there was a man who was the 'head of the home' and his opening sentence to me was "Hello Lizzy, I know all about you, you're trouble and I am not putting up with any of your antics here". I was angry (ashamed) and hurt, I literally walked in one door and straight out another, I stayed away for 6 weeks which in those days was the longest time anyone had absconded, (with little else achieved in my life, I was proud of this!) I slept rough, in barns, under bridges, Jetty's until I met up with a group of 'punks' who were squatting in derelict houses, I stayed with them and they were really good to me, they looked after me and were never inappropriate or abusive. The police visited a couple of times looking for me and so at my request the 'punks' shaved off my hair into a Mohican style, afterwards I actually showed police who were looking for me, around the house, as they asked me if I had seen me! To my impoverished sense of self, this was another achievement.

When I did return to the home, I was 14, almost 15 years old, I knew I only had another year left (in those days we left residential care at 16) and so I needed to 'knuckle down' and do the best I can for my own future. I also knew that any more absconding and I would be sent to a secure unit and that I had narrowly escaped this already.

The way in which children and young people are received when they return from absconding / missing episodes, is of huge importance, I once worked with some lovely foster carers who would always greet children with a cup of hot chocolate and a hug (where appropriate), they would also sit up all night with young people, nurturing and reassuring them as they 'came down' from taking drugs, because they recognised the important message to young people that it was 'safe' to return home. I have since used and developed this model of care further in my delivery of fostering services.

Despite the difficult start at the children's home when I first arrived, this was to be the best placement I ever lived, and I took away some invaluable and positive life lessons and to this day I remain in contact with some of the staff.

Therefore, before I move forward in this chapter and cite some of the 'less positive' examples that have informed my own professional practice, I wish to reiterate that this was prior to the Children Act 1989 and I believe that generally, people working unqualified in residential childcare had good intentions, although they did not have access to the training, knowledge and insight that has emerged since.

A memorable and poignant moment was when on a day out with everyone from the children's home, I sat alone on a hilltop with the 'head of the home' and he looked at me and asked me 'what can I do to make you happy?' I replied 'I just want to see my sisters' and he seemed genuinely sad as he told me that was the one thing he could not do for me. Despite his often-obvious frustrations with me, in that moment I allowed myself to believe that he really did care about me and that he knew I was simply unhappy. ......And just maybe, I could bring myself to consider that he even liked me! Years later I learned how hard he fought (without success) on my behalf for me to be able to see my sisters, he too had been angry and saddened by my situation, although I never knew that at the time, and I frequently took my rage out on him (and other staff).

I never really understood why I was not able to have contact with my sisters and I had no idea where they were and for most of the time where my mum was either, the only thing that was obvious to me was that there was something wrong with me, I was 'bad' and that's why 'bad' things happened to me.

Informed by my experiences in care, when working with children and young people I have always tried to be honest and transparent and if I did not have the answers, I would admit that. I have tried hard never to judge and to think carefully about the conversations I have, recognising the power of insensitive / unintended comments to reinforce negative ideas that children may have internalised about themselves. It is essential to a child's recovery and ability to move forward for them to have a narrative about their history and circumstances that makes sense to them, all too often professionals do not have enough knowledge, insight or confidence to be able to discuss and share information with the children that they are working with or caring for.

In my own practice and my management of staff, I am committed to ensuring and facilitating meaningful contact and discussions with children, and make sure that separation and endings are necessary and sensitive, thoughtful and understood. I ensure that practitioners undertaking 'life story' work with children are appropriately trained and supported including those staff that are supervising contact between children and their families. All too often these activities are process driven and undertaken without due thought and consideration to the practitioner's capacity to bear and contain the pain and unconscious dynamics inherent within the room. I am also aware that these matters have the potential to be my greatest 'bear trap' and so I am mindful of the complexities of my own experiences and use supervision effectively to maintain a balance if appropriate and to consider my own unconscious bias. I have been fortunate to have had access to good quality clinical supervision and training during most of my career and can generally reflect upon and interpret my responses to the work.

One Christmastime, I recall over hearing staff complaining about having to work on Christmas day because I was the only child with nowhere else to go, not only was this a painful reminder that my mum was only a short walking distance away and that she did not want me, not even to see me, but what they never realised is that I also registered that in previous years when it had been just one child remaining, staff took them home with them, so their comments reinforced my belief that (without doubt) I was bad and not liked. Although I must add that every member of staff that came on duty that Christmas brought presents for me and cooked my favourite food, without even discussing it and of their own accord, one of the other young people returned early to see me, it was and still is my best Christmas ever!

The staff working in the home did not understand that children and young people hear everything, and what they cannot hear, they imagine / fantasize / second guess, because for children and young people who have experienced trauma and abuse, this is a coping mechanism, a well-developed method of defence to keep themselves safe and to avoid further attack, situations out of their control.

I did not help myself because I coped with pain and rejection by being angry, argumentative, and presenting with an "I don't give a f**k" attitude, I was defending myself from being hurt again. I absconded regularly and subsequently, my reputation was not good, (I was bad) and I was always 'in trouble'. Once when some of the younger children absconded, I bumped into them and I told them it was too cold to stay out and I walked them back home and then carried on out myself, when I returned I was 'in trouble' because the staff believed I had encouraged those younger children to 'run away'! These types of situations (of which there were many) filled me with rage at the injustice and I would respond accordingly, with anger and afterwards I would feel embarrassed and full of self-loathing.

Frequently, I was told that I would 'turn out just like my

Mum'. I never fully comprehended what that meant but deep down I knew she was 'loose' and in their minds immoral and I assumed that is what they were saying about me, what they never knew was that due to my earlier childhood experiences, I was far from being promiscuous, the idea was abhorrent to me, their comments induced shame. Even at a young age, I appreciated that my mum had also grown up in care and gave birth to me at the age of 16, I never knew what happened to her except that her siblings were also 'in care' as were my cousins, deep inside I understood that something about my mum's life was sad, and she had lived a difficult childhood too. I had huge and deep-rooted empathy and loyalty towards my mum, no matter what she did.

In my work with foster carers and staff and directly with children and young people, I emphasise the importance of avoiding any type of transference from personal or professional feelings and opinions about children and young people and their family members. I appreciate why children mostly remain loyal and protective of their parents' as it is far less painful to assume that there is something lacking in them than to think that their parents are accountable or do not love them. In my own experience it was easier to forgive and excuse my mum's behaviour than my own.

Weekends, when the 'head of the home' and his wife were not working, almost always ended with me being told I would be 'in trouble' when they returned (for some misdemeanour or another). My bravado and nonchalant attitude, as if I did not care, was a defence and coping mechanism and those comments evoked my anxiety, waiting for them to come on duty, also reinforced negative feelings, and associated behaviours, sometimes I would abscond to avoid their return and to take control over 'my troubles'. Similarly, children in care are already pre-disposed to 'taking the blame' and feeling deficient, and it is important not to presume wrongdoings and to manage sanctions appropriately and timely, this is especially relevant in fostering and residential settings.

I knew that staff recorded information about everything we did and to this day, I sometimes experience paranoia thinking about if people are talking about me, and what they are saying (always presumed negative) and I relate this to being in care, where everything about you is written down. Recording is perhaps a necessary evil, and in my own written documents and when quality assuring others, I ensure and offer guidance with regards to the accuracy and sensitivity of the content and rationale. I urge professionals and carers to share their recording with children and young people, encouraging them to contribute as doing so, may facilitate opportunities for reflection, learning and healing. Records should be an important memoir of a child's journey through care and professionals must consider what they have written recognising that it will possibly be revisited at a much later date, including when the child is an adult. It is vital to refrain from using jargon, judgments and narratives that will reinforce negative inner working models. In the absence of a loving family to recount memories, children or adults looking back and reading their files should stimulate a feeling that they were, or are, cared for and thought about with sincerity and kindness.

Having settled down in the home I began attending school regularly and with clean and modern uniform, and the provision of regular meals, I was able to engage properly with my education. Having a clean and full PE kit enabled me to enjoy participating in sports at school as well as performing arts, I realised that my dream was to become a dancer; I had never taken dance lessons and was self-taught (this was the age of break dancing!) I loved music and dancing with a passion, it was therapeutic (although I did not understand that at the time). I was most fortunate to have a PE teacher in my final year at school that recognised my talent and supported me, encouraging me to audition for a performing arts college, which I did and was accepted.

My audition was in another town, that I had never been to before, and some distance away. I had not seen my social worker again since being placed back in the home and so I asked the staff to speak to him and requested that he took me to my audition, to my pleasure (and surprise) he agreed. However, the evening before I was informed that he could not take me, I was hugely disappointed (worried and anxious) and I demonstrated my feelings through anger. I had a terrible row with the wife (of the head of the home) and when she pushed me, I pushed her back, thankfully she was not hurt. The following morning, I travelled on the bus by myself to the audition. When I returned, I was told I needed to leave, and so I was placed in lodgings aged 16 years. I was very happy living independently and not only did I attend college, but I also had a part time catering job, I had freedom, money, I looked after myself, dressed well and was very happy. My happiness was short lived when my landlady's mother became unwell and they needed the room back to care for her, I tried to contact my old social worker, without success. I recall sitting at the end of my landlady's path, on my suitcase with nowhere to live, I had no clue what I would do or where I would go.

I returned to squatting and at the same time I met someone, we fell in love, and he joined me living at the squat. Predictably I became pregnant at the age of 18 years, by which time I had dropped out of college. When my son was born I looked at him, I asked myself if this is what love feels like, and I knew that I would never ever let anything bad happen to him. I reflected upon my own experiences with my mum, and I could not understand why she allowed those things to happen to me and my sisters. I knew I would spend the rest of my life protecting and taking good care of my son. By the time he was a year old, we were housed in one of the worst housing estates in the area. I knew that for him to have a better chance than I had at life, I needed to get us out of that estate. I knew the only way out was to get a mortgage and buy a house and to do that I needed a career. I sat and pondered, I literally had no idea whatsoever about anything that I was good at and that I could progress as a career, I knew I could not return to dancing with a baby, and then it came to me, "I know what it is like to be a teenager in care and misunderstood."

I applied to a local university and was invited to attend an interview with a panel of professionals. I thought that I recognised one of the panel members and was thankful that I had applied using my formal name Elizabeth and the surname that was on my birth certificate, which was given to me when I had officially left care. Prior to which I had been known by multiple surnames as my mum moved around, living with one guy after another, taking their names and changing ours. The interview went as well as might be expected given I was a 19-year-old without any appropriate work experience or the required qualifications and I was given some helpful advice to apply again when I was older and had gained relevant work experience. I had omitted to refer to my previous care experience and as I left the room, the panel member I vaguely recognised said out loud to me and in front of everyone else; "I suppose I should refer to you as Lizzy XXXX" (previous surname). The blood rushed to my head, I wanted the ground to open up and swallow me as I felt the shame of being recognised and referred to by my 'old' surname wash over me. I did not understand, nor did I question why I should feel such shame, just that I did and it was overwhelming. I was mortified. I never wanted to pursue a career in social work again, for fear of being recognised and exposed.

Shortly afterwards I met a senior manager from the local authority, she was lovely and we had an honest conversation about my experience at interview and my plans. She was supportive and she advised me to continue but never to tell anyone that I was 'in care', explaining other peoples' views about 'skeletons in my closet' if things go wrong. The way in which I interpreted and internalised this statement has stayed with me throughout my career and for many years, the vast majority of my career, I never told anyone.

I studied A' levels part time whilst working and in the absence of any other ideas, I decided I would continue with my plan to be a social worker and that I would not apply to study or work locally, or where anyone would recognise me.

Whilst I was a student social worker I was in placement at a homeless shelter and I came across someone I had lived with in a children's home, I knew that she had gone on to have a terrible adulthood with frequent periods imprisoned. I was really pleased to see her, I wanted to hug her and speak to her properly and ask her about her life but again I felt humiliated and uncomfortable when she recognised me and from one end of the corridor to the other, she shouted out my full name (including previous surname) greeting me with joy, once again I wanted the ground to open up and swallow me.

I rarely told anyone for the first 20 years of my career that I was once a looked after child, and only a very small minority who became my closest confidantes after many years.

In 2003, I was most fortunate to be part of a team in the local authority implementing the Leaving Care Act. I welcomed this legislation because I knew from experience how it felt to leave care too soon, become homeless, drop out of education, teenage pregnancy with no adults to guide or support me. I met almost every criteria for why this legislation was crucial for young people leaving care. When I was asked to manage the team I did not perceive this request as recognition of my hard work and dedication, I was petrified that this would be the moment when I would be exposed as a fraud, a failure and everybody would learn that I was not worthy and indeed incompetent. My manager at the time (somebody to whom I continue to have enormous respect and gratitude) told me that "as the most senior person in the team I had no choice but to 'act up' as the team manager." Had I not been put in such a position, I probably would never have had the courage to embrace the role and those managerial roles that followed.

Since qualifying I have been naturally predisposed to working with and developing services for those children and young people with the most complex and challenging needs and this has ignited my passion for learning about attachment, neuroscience, resilience and understanding how trauma manifests through behaviour, interpreting how children communicate their experiences of trauma and abuse through their behaviour. Ever since I have been utterly committed and encouraging of professionals including foster carers to apply similar curiosity, and not to be judgmental or labelling which may facilitate negative self-fulfilling prophecies.

I continue to use insight based upon my experiences and learning every day and to better equip me with managing staff, change and service delivery. I have found this to be especially valuable during times when staff encounter difficulties, are avoidant and lacking in motivation. I explain the significance of their work in direct relation to the experiences of looked after children, for example meeting a key performance indicator is not a 'tick-box' number crunching exercise but an opportunity to move closer to achieving a positive outcome for a child and the significance of maintaining compliance as being more than an onerous task.

Once a service was resistant to relocation and consumed with anxiety, I encouraged individuals to consider how it might feel for children and young people moving between placements, loosing important information, phone numbers, addresses and their fear of what is not known.

Informed by my own experience of being in care, I pioneered therapeutic foster care and I have a passionate interest and commitment to the provision of high quality, sustainable and reparative placements, inspired by my personal and professional insight into the immense importance of stable and secure placements to promote the physical and emotional needs of looked after children and young people, because without placement stability and quality foster care their prognosis becomes increasingly deprived.

Lately, being 'care experienced' seems to be acceptable and I have tentatively become more open about sharing that I was once a care leaver, although I am sceptical and not convinced that disclosing such personal information is always met appropriately and without judgment.

Recently a manager openly referred to difficulties that another social worker was experiencing (of a similar age to me) as being caused by her having unresolved issues because she had been 'looked after'. I politely reminded him of my own status and questioned, professionally, his rationale. After I told another manager about my care experience status, it was referenced at every occasion that we met for supervision and over time I began to question and doubt myself.

Initially I was reluctant and (I realise) avoidant to contributing to this book, however I am indebted to Mary whose persistence has facilitated an opportunity for me to reflect, and to look back over my career and recognise that whilst I have always been a most powerful advocate for children, young people and other professionals, the times when I have been most ineffective and unable to challenge professional 'injustice' and poor practice has been when it is directed at me, when as a practitioner or manager I have been treated unfairly, inappropriately or unprofessionally and despite knowing a situation is wrong, I have felt powerless to make an appropriate challenge. My confidence slowly corrodes as my instinct is always to focus upon my own perceived failings and I have become more concerned about being seen as a 'troublemaker' than advocating on my own behalf. This is in spite of the knowledge that I am generally well respected and held in high regard by my colleagues and peers. On one occasion I have even resigned from an organisation rather than to challenge or draw attention to the poor practice and unprofessionalism of senior management.

Looking back at my time in care, I would not change a thing, when I was a child somebody once told me that living with disadvantage and misfortune was character building. I believe they were right. I feel blessed that my experiences have provided me with a wealth of insight and material that I have been able to use effectively to genuinely make a positive difference to the lives of many children. Along the way I have had the immense good fortune and privilege to work alongside and to learn from some amazing and inspirational people. I conclude having learned that the only trouble with me, is my crippling insecurities and self-doubt, and the legacy of being a 'troublemaker' that continues to haunt me.

The invisible bridge

- Ian Dickson

I don't have many childhood memories. For me as a child, care in the 1950's/60's was merely a state to be endured until I was big enough and old enough to escape and not be a child any longer.

Childhood was a time of being a very small minnow in an ocean full of hostile sharks, circling and ever watchful for signs of weakness so that they might attack. Each day was a challenge to be survived and a fight to stay one step ahead of the "staff" and other kids to ensure you got a share. Nobody really wanted a photograph of that.

That was the care system of the post war decades, a time when abuse in care settings was commonplace and harsh and genuine love and care were at a premium. Children were "done to" not "done with".

Back then in the English care system, staff were too often the enemy, not to be trusted, and sometimes even to be hated. They came and went, staying in your life for a while and then suddenly gone, and another new staff "face" appeared to take their place and earn your fear and hatred.

Social workers played their part too. They were more distant figures, less immediately threatening and not hated. They were feared and distrusted though. They were rarely seen and had little impact on daily life, but their appearance usually meant trouble or change, bad news or yet another move. They were messengers of the unwelcome, a warning that something or somebody was about to be lost or taken away.

Although sometimes feared, social workers were not usually as despised as some of the less popular staff or carers – they were very rarely if ever directly involved in abusing you, nor did they usually humiliate or embarrass you in front of others, but they were to be distrusted, as part of "them". One did not show weakness in front of them or tell them anything. Most importantly, one must never like them.

As a child I spent almost 16 years in care. These defensive attitudes were part of my daily life and shared with every other kid in care I met. It was "us" and "them" and "them" definitely included social workers. Those attitudes travelled with me into adulthood when I left care and cosily buried themselves deep into my unconscious memory, arising every now and again when triggered by some incident or recollection. Like the letters in a stick of Blackpool rock, they were an integral part of who I was. They had been part of my survival kit and belief set that enabled me to cope with the daily terrors of being a frightened child in a care system perceived by all I knew as hostile and threatening.

As long as "we" remained defiant and unbroken and never opened up to "them", we were strong, and they could not hurt us. Even if we were desperately frightened and unhappy.

Many care experienced people will remember those feelings with a wry smile. Harmlessly resting in memory, they are just background music as life in care and the care system become increasingly historical in the daily business of living.

So, it was for me. In the years after care, I put a defiant two fingers up to care, carers, and social workers and settled down, married, had a family got on with family life. I trained towards becoming an industrial chemist and my future was mapped out. But I was bored with the predictable daily routine of the laboratory. I wanted a more challenging career. I looked towards social work.

Social work was an obvious career choice. After all, had I not spent 16 years in care and seen and learned lots of things about being in care and the care system? Was I not one of "us"? I could relate to the children in care and understand them, they would relate to me and together we could really sort their lives out. I was an "expert" and could show children how to survive as I did. Having spent so long in care I confidently believed that I knew all the answers.

So, I became a social worker. One of the first things I learned was that I did not know all the answers. In fact, I was not even aware of all the questions! I wanted to reach out and embrace the children in care. I wanted to reassure them that I was one of them and I would get them through this if they put their trust in me.... if they put their trust in me. Aye, there's the rub as one much brighter than I once said. I spent years in care learning never to trust or put faith in social workers – they would only let you down. Now here was I, suddenly expecting other children to trust me. How does that work?

In reality, I did not have a magic wand. I did not have the time, energy, resource or if I'm honest, inclination to be able to deliver on the needs and wants of every child I worked with. I was just another cog in a bigger system churning away. Wheels within wheels with managers and politicians hidden in the shadows, directing so many of my decisions.

How could I, knowing what I know, honestly ask any child in care to trust me? How could I ask them to ignore the survival skills that being in care had taught them and ask them to be vulnerable to an adult stranger just because he happened to have once many years ago been in care too? I was an expert by experience, but that was MY care experience, not theirs.

I usually got on with kids I worked with. I always did my best for them and don't think any of them hated me, but I am not sure how many of them trusted me as a social worker either. At the end of the day, I was a social worker. And social workers are not to be trusted. Them's the rules!

Having been in care and having care experience does not simply bring ready answers and simple solutions to the care experienced social worker. I am confident that it can bring insights and offer a window to glance into the world of the child in care usually hidden from the view of officialdom. But it does NOT bring that magic wand.

Being a care experienced social worker and working with children in care will not of itself provide us with any answers or provide a short circuit for children to pass swiftly through the hardships that care can bring or towards contentment, fulfilment or being at peace with themselves.

Being care experienced and working in social work simply reminds us of the very obvious fact that children in care are normal! They are literally like us. They are usually ordinary kids who have found themselves in extraordinary circumstances and adapted to survive – as we did. I recall one of my brothers was described on his care file as "maladjusted". He is now one of Scotland's successful artists, a happily married man with a loving family. Creative, intelligent, caring, reflective – but not maladjusted. Never maladjusted. He was very well adjusted indeed for the care setting he found himself in. I hope as a care experienced social worker, that was an awareness my own experiences gave to me.

Being a care experienced social worker, with a wide range of care experienced friends and peers, reminds me daily what a creative diverse, intelligent, caring and truly generous community the care community is.

Care experienced people are found amongst all the great artists, sportspeople, scientists, philosophers, doctors and writers. There are many amongst some great plumbers, electricians, bus drivers, factory workers – and social workers – too. Being care experienced teaches us that the care experience can last a lifetime, but it is not a life sentence. We are not defined by it or restricted by it.

That is the message I have tried to share with young people in care that I have worked with. I have never denied my care experience or kept it quiet as some sort of "dark secret", which it is not. I have used my care experience when I felt it could help children much as I might use DIY skills to support them – if I had any.

I may not have any simple solutions or the magic wand, but I do have me as living proof that we are not bound by our history or heritage. That we can achieve our dreams with self-belief, hard work, opportunity and the wit to take advantage of that opportunity.

I can point children in care to the many care experienced people all around them who have made their mark on their own lives and society. I can show them where there may be choices that they can make. Their lives may be hard and may not improve quickly enough, but they CAN do it as I did, and others do every day. They need to believe in themselves and have hope, determination and optimism. That is only step one of course. Those young people need the resource and opportunity to make their dreams happen.

That is the other side of being a care experienced social worker. We are morally and ethically bound in my view to campaign to ensure those young people get those resources and opportunities to enable them to cross the invisible bridge between care and ordinary life in the wider community.

Let's make that invisible bridge visible so that one day every child in care can cross. That must be our ambition.

The message sent is not always the message received.

- Virginia Satir

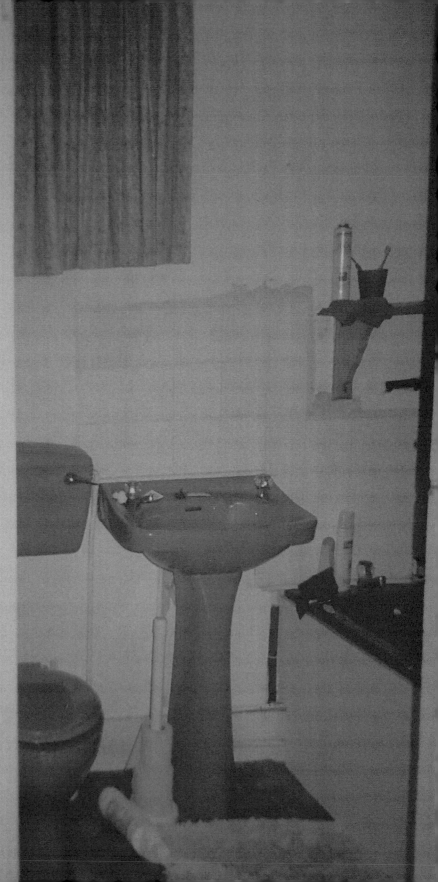

POETRY

Frown Lines and Bruised Minds

- Saira-Jayne Jones

My face is a map traced with journeys.

Happenings endured with time.

The climbs of arduous mountains, the beds of rivers I've cried.

History etched into every line, every furrow and crease of my brow.

Events that have long since faded leave an ache in the here and now.

Shame secreted in shadows, horrors hidden from view.

My eyes a glimpse into depths of despair, where my once innocence became skewed.

My face keeps all of my secrets, only in its reflection revealed.

A battle to express my distress, adorn my cheeks with the pain that I feel.

Each ridge of flesh each deepened fold.

Reflect meanderings of memories, of the fears that I hold.
With passing years my face grows old.

Beneath lives a burning reminder of everything they stole.

My face no longer compliant no longer told or controlled.
Now I'm the one with the power to tell.

To share all the stories I hold.

Where I Stand

- Saira-Jayne Jones

Just a child
That's all I was
A small...scared...confused human
What I needed was your love.

I needed to feel like I mattered
That my thinks and my feels were enough
I needed to feel safe and protected
When my world was chaotic, and things became tough

When I stood with tears burning my cheeks
My stomach, folding itself into knots
All I wanted, was to be able to speak
When my eyes met with yours, contempt's what I got.

Where I stood seemed so distant, so far away
I felt I'd be taken by the wind or tide
Of all the anguish and suffering, I now kept from the world
Sealed away, locked deep down inside

My words became lost in the turmoil and pain
Diluted by tears and washed from my brain...
My thoughts consuming themselves
Where I stood, now became the place that I knelt

I was just a child
All's I wanted to know was why?
When you're a child, you should feel loved, safe, and happy...
I felt bereft, I felt trapped, dead inside

No longer standing, I was dejected, crumpled and angry
I knelt at your feet like a slave
I cried, and I begged your forgiveness,
I longed for embrace, instead you sent me away.

I was collected like an unwanted parcel
Not the kind you handle with care
My edges already battered and dented
My return was inevitable, as was their despair.

When I stood in the office, awaiting your car
My life shoved in bin liners, my heart crushed and scarred
I needed someone to see me, to care enough to hold space,
Instead, what I got was your vitriol, bungled off in your
Peugeot... to yet another strange place.

My life is now punctuated with losses
An overdose of pain, blame and shame
That's punctured holes through my person
Left unanswered questions, strewn in their wake

There are too many places where I've stood and cried
When I was a child, I never quite felt one inside
I had to tackle the world through adult eyes
Still, I stood with questions, just too many why's

Shipped and stripped of my knowing,
My essence... faded away
My tree with its branches, stripped of its leaves
My puzzle, its pieces, in complete disarray

Transported to my next destination
Despite my protesting and much consternation
I was the unwanted child, feral and too hard to place
Where I stood, bags in hand and heart pounding, you looked
upon my brokenness with pure disdain.

This place was very different... the adults not parents, now
staff
Where I now stood at 15 was at the edge of a cliff
The realisation I am now by myself...
Alone

Undeserving of the time and love of a family,
Now I'm just a name on a board
My comings and goings my thinks and my feels,
All noted down, in continuous record

I needed to find all my answers
Where I now stood, was in the unknown
Too many voids in my timeline
The why's... all I wanted to know

When I was cast away from your shackles
I had to go it alone
With the gaps you had left in my person
Sink or swim... never expecting that I'd stay afloat

My navigation skills weren't very effective
I got side-tracked down many scary dead ends
Nobody there to help me co-pilot through storms
To take the reins when things were running away

I had been left with fragments and battle scars
Ones I was unable to hide
I wrangled to understand them
From where I stood, there were still too many why's

I contemplated many directions
Explored rabbit holes in the maze of my mind
I would stand and attempt to make sense of it all
The answers evaded me...information denied.

I thought I'd find out from the inside
There must be some secret truth
That keeps me locked in the unknowing
Privileges you with the answers I sought

I never disclosed my road map
What had bought me to this place
Where I stood, and what developed my passions
Why I needed to exist in this space

I strived to obtain what I needed
To be able to make sense of my world
Whilst in this process of doing
I realised that with my why's, I could maybe do more...

I had to seek many solutions,
To overcome barriers and gaps
Replace pieces that had become missing,
Develop a greater sense of myself

Where I stood was complex and tricky
One foot on each side of the fence
My perspective always seemed a bit different
For my contributions, I was rarely thanked

I exhausted myself in pursuit of answers, to inform my judgements and decisions
I delivered my tasks with all my heart, executed with the upmost precision
I bent over backwards to demonstrate my worth, in this unfit for purpose system
I stood there subjected to further raised eyebrows, contempt, doubt, and awkward suspicion.

I was viewed with deficiency, that my past would affect my propensity for reliable connection
Never mind my first-class honours degree, and distinctions for my two practice placements
I couldn't be a professional in their view, my background would apparently dictate
Too much vested interest, too assertive for the rights of the people to whom I'm not supposed to relate.

I stood and tried to make sense of the entire situation
That the values I'd studied, internalised, ascribed to, were somehow in contention
Everything I stood for incongruent, with this budget led unaccountable profession
The people at the centre, no more than a number on a ledger, their needs an expensive distraction

I took a stand against the malaise, that I had witnessed since my social work inception
I was fighting against the tide, from the other side, pushed and pulled in different directions
The environment was a challenge, it became difficult for me to remain
Because despite many others agreeing, that things were not right, when I spoke up, I was stood by myself once again.

I was trying so very hard to move mountains,
Until realising it can begin with small stones
The ripples in water that gradually become waves,
They don't happen at once, they build up, their strength grows.

The small seeds that we plant, become blooms, that nurture an abundance of hope
A new day upon the horizon, developing relationships, supporting people to reach for their goals
Going forward with passion, determination, and heart
With the confidence and commitment that I can be the difference, because it's with the small stuff it starts.

The art of life & chaos

- Narges Qauyumi

We all play part in what feels like
an endless game of chess
Remember life cheats us all.

I am who I am, and that will always be enough.
Our paths will cross whilst we walk different lives
but our experience will be what we share
amongst the chaos we refer to as life.

Our mind, body, and soul connected as one
bringing stability like yin and yang.
Life's chaos will conceal your identity.
Embrace that which you are hiding from
and you'll learn to embrace your truth

Happiness isn't a given experience
But rather a state of being.
Remember we are all dysfunctional beings.

Adapted because we must

- David Grimm

We are the seeds
the wild wind sews,
torn from the ground and thrown,
placed in arenas that weren't quite our own...
Yet we thrive,
yet we grow.

Though strange and distinct,
No resemblance in sight,
We assimilate,
Overcome,
And adapt to all that might challenge our life.

We refuse to fall,
Refuse to kneel,
Shattered by the wind, yet
United... we rise.
Always bold, always worthy of delight,
Still ready for the growth, ready ...
For the endless fight.

We will never be torn,
we've taken the land,
and made it our own.

Hero Worship

- David Grimm

I don't think you know.

You were the person that saved my soul,
Took my hands, broken, shattered, wrinkled by deluge after
deluge of tears.
You gave me hope that the sun might shine,
The world may turn, and my smile recur cemented eternal.

You could have tempered my fear with caring concern,
A whisper of support. Even a padded lie...
But you chose to stay formal,
You chose to evade.
Chose to stay away,
And leave me Fearful.

With boundaries in place you crushed my belief,
I'm sorry I stressed you and laboured your time,
I didn't know you were human,
With feelings and more,

I believed you a suit, sent to protect me,
Like that of a knight in a fight for his life.

Thank you for saving me, from so much more,
And for protecting yourself from my
Misplaced, mistimed, friendship.

At what cost?

- David Grimm

I
Don't
Even
Know
Who
I
Am.

You shuffled me from harm,
Moving my body and mind,
But you left my heart in danger
Under threat from those
With hate inside.

I found it later, broken and torn.
Squashed between the spaces
In a thousand piece jigsaw puzzle.

They taught me how to sew
In your place of safety,
So I took each ripped and ragged piece
And slowly replaced the piece of me
That you couldn't save,
that no money could replace,
no allowance, paper or time could mirror the motions,
that once spurred on my soul.

You should have left me to fry.

I have never been the same ,
the jigsaw never quite fit together,
and the rhythm of my heart is now a guessing game,
there is no camber, no thumping beat.
Where they were once connected,
My heart and mind now march to the rhythms of separate
songs,
One a string quartet,
The other...and anarchistic rave scene.

And
I
Don't
Know
Who
I
Am
So I'll guess and guess until I find a way.

Humpty Dumpty

- David Grimm

I will be.
What you failed to be...
The reason they smile when old,
and I'm a long gone.

You were a saviour,
A champion,
A giant in my tiny land.

Though not your intention, with your cold,
Hardened and broken "smile"... you moulded a knight,
With the shimmer of sunshine and a overwhelming darkness.
Though I'm not your child, you have raised within me,
the strength and resolve to embrace what is right,
to challenge injustice and to share the light.

I will be. What you failed to be...an agent for good,
In a darkened, and lost life.

Language of Deficit

- David Grimm

I try to be positive,
A mind of creation,
Of endless optimism,
Bordering on annoying.

The type of man that has to calm,
Or his own energy will drive him round the bend.
I try to be a smile, a welcome sight,
In a sea of darkness I try to be a flickering light.

But the language you taught me,
Was that of deficit,
Can't do this...
Can't do that...
Never will be...
Why should I try?

I endeavour to lead a life that others might like,
To challenge your voice, as it sits on my mind.
To live a way that sets example to others,
Hoping to inspire ambition in those that you have infested,
With your language of deficit.

I hope when you see us,
Tackling the world with purses full of sun,
your negatives flee and you smile at the sight,
so many of your kids made it through the system,
with love in their hearts and hope in their eyes...

You accept the love you think you deserve

- Anon

I continue to carry and hold the blame
My head still floods with heavy shame
Guilt, rejection and pain
It's effected the right side of my brain.
My ability to build healthy relationships hindered
This trauma that remains lingered
Started in my childhood
And continued through my adulthood.

A broken smile hidden even to those that knew me the most.
Commenting on my upbeat nature and captivating glow.
A master at shielding my vulnerability,
Hidden by my humour,
If only they knew,
How much I was struggling to get through
There was those that were persistent, watching with their wise eyes,
Who begun to dig deep, questioning the never ending cobweb of lies.
My ability to emulate happiness and present so well
Meant people would accept the stories I would tell.
Be open, it will get better, be persistent you will stay safe,
It created a case, but this led to no proper base.
You felt betrayed, I was left feeling more afraid.

You promised that you would keep me safe and be the only one that would ever want me
Told me not to trust anyone that is claiming to be a helping hand.
They don't care about you, you would say, they will give up on you, he laughed, everything continued to happen so fast.

My world collapsed in so many ways,
The fear will never be forgotten
The imprint left on my mind, brain and body, will forever feel
rotten.
The randomers you got to hurt me is something that will
always stay,
I hold hope and I pray that you are now where you deserve
to stay
In order to survive I denied my true self to be known.
In order to have some form of peace I continuously put
myself down.
In order to silence my internal pain, I pushed others away,
But I now know the right ones will always stay.

You may of took everything I had,
You can break everything I am,
Beat me down to nothing,
But I continue rise, I learn and I grow.

My trauma didn't make me "stronger"
It made me weak, unable to speak
Memory loss and sleepless nights
Distressed, overwhelmed and easily startled
BUT, wiser, more compassionate, more loving and finally
free.

You accept the love you think you deserve.

From care to where: The social workee becomes the social worker

- Mike. S

From second guessing
And thinking: 'how depressing'

From another session
With another question

Successions
And oppressions
And suppressing aggression

For what
For when
For who
For me

To become an expert
Of experience
Of myself
Trying to master progression

Expert of what

Learning and loving theory and methods
Wealth of life in possession
Life stories behold
To be told and untold

And then to focus on helping others

The passion
An obsession

Still carrying stories that are unknown and unheard

Remember to forget
And remember to stop
Stop repressing
And start confessing

Find expression
But with discretion

Fear comes
With uncertainty
Blame then shame
Find forgiveness in me
Hunt for healing
Sharing and not scaring
It's all about what we bring

No transgression
Make a real impression
Despite the micro-aggression
From care to where
Everything is a lesson
Don't lessen your worth
In a real and raw, worthwhile profession

From care to where: My mum wasn't sure about my career choice

- Mike. S

"Traitor"
"Betrayer"
"Judas"
And "Snake"

"Backstabber"
"Sell-out"
"Rat"
And "Snitch"

"Defector"
"Deserter"
"Turncoat"
And "Informant"

Stop social working me said my mum to me...

If only my peers knew my fears
If only they knew how I grew
I had lots on my plate
And now work for the state
Helping families to simply get through

*

Social workers who grow up in care
Live childhoods that seem quite unfair
They move about quite a lot
Can tie their life story in knots
But the insights they have are quite rare

- Mike. S

The Cliff Edge

- Rebekah Pierre

No man is an island, or so it's been said
That we're sociable creatures, community-led
And we need one another, no matter how much
We might like to make out that we don't need a 'crutch'.

From the moment we're born we're dependent on others
We live among guardians, fathers or mothers
Can't fend for ourselves, we're in need of protection
And when we're much older require direction.

No matter our age or how much we have grown
We need those kind words at the end of a phone
Just someone to talk to when hardships at bay
When we've had some bad news, or a really shit day

And the opposite's true when our life's going well
We need someone to cheer for us, someone to tell
About course grades or jobs, even finding the one
A person to celebrate things we have done

But beyond joy and sorrow there's much in-between
The humdrum of life that so oft goes unseen
Like mundane life admin, insurance and tax
Things on which google is painfully lax

It helps to be able to reach out and ask,
When you're not getting far with some DIY task
There's no handbook to life and we're not born all-knowing
We don't have the answers to everything going

But for us CEP there is no guarantee
That there's someone to call on (at least with no fee)
When we just need a sounding board, help or advice
Others take this for granted, don't even think twice.

Much has been said of the cliff edge of care
When you wake up one morning and nobody's there
But people don't talk of the opposite side
How to scale it again with no compass or guide

We start from ground zero whilst others it seems
Are up in the mountains in well-equipped teams
Reaching dizzying heights, we watch as they soar
And we yearn for a world with a more even score

For if we should fall there is no safety net
No home to go back to, no place to reset
There are studies that show what we must overcome -
Loss, stigma and poverty naming just some

Or poorer health outcomes no matter our ages
Names written on charge sheets not academic pages
And constant reminders of what we may 'LAC'
In a world where we're sold things in 'family pack'.

Where we turn on the telly and all we can see
Are 2.4 children in close family
At Christmas, Hanukkah, Diwali or Eid
It's hard to dodge questions which usually lead

'What are your plans, with whom are you staying?'
And you spend the whole time just sitting there praying
That the topic will change before it's your turn
To some other matter, some other concern

Diversity matters, seen and unseen
But CEP voices are caught in-between
I rarely disclose, it's less hassle to hide
To shelve this identity off to the side

We need recognition, quite how I'm not sure
So that stigma and shame will define us no more
I long for the day I can share it with pride
When our past does not contribute to a divide

But excuse me one moment for I must digress
To speak of a system in such a big mess
I promised myself that I'd change it, you see
When I went into social work (what naïveté!)

I thought I could be who I needed in care
Someone steadfast, compassionate, competent, fair
But with cutbacks and years of austerity
The caseloads increased with severity

My intentions were good but it wasn't enough
For to fix a whole system is awfully tough
It needs proper investment from those at the top
(Not lukewarm pledges like world leaders at COP)

The government's failing, it's massively screwed
Over families who live without shelter or food
With benefits always the first to be axed
Yet there's billionaires who have never been taxed

In a world where what matters is financial gain
We must never tire, never cease to campaign
To put rights before pound signs and care before cost
Lest more CEP lives become needlessly lost

With privatisation comes risk of great harm
To children not able to sound an alarm
We must be their voice for if not us then who?
Yes you know the answer - it's starting with you.

Assessed and Supported Year in Employment

- Anon

I started off my ASYE
Feeling competent, capable
And compassion fatigue.
Championed for being
an all-rounded hero
Care-experienced, Fostering
A social worker, just so you know.

Three months into my ASYE
I felt coerced into seeing OT
My workload fell behind you see
So, they gave me some actions
To help bring me in line

Another day another week,
My supervisor says six months in
You're not where you're meant to be!
Do you know what this could mean?
I mean an extension possibly
But capabilities seriously?

Six months into my ASYE
Feeling demotivated, doubtful,
And at times distressed.
I had never met anxiety
until encountering this stress!

Halfway through, I don't know what comes next!
I don't even know how I got into this mess!
Don't challenge, keep your head down!
Just do as you're told!
If you're lucky you might go unnoticed!
Because you've got six months more to go!

ESSAYS

Anti-oppressive practice is not an intellectual activity

- Ian Thomas

Is there a static social truth, or are we all interpreting a subjective reality that has no real veracity? This is an important question for social work and anti-oppressive practice. There are some clear facts which we must be accountable to. For example, assessing risk and keeping people safe. However, it is my observation that intellectualising social work can be a barrier to emotional astuteness, and therefore anti-oppressive practice. We must transcend traditional models of reflection; REAL connection involves journeying to meet ourselves through introspective emotional enquiry! Here lies the divine where humanness is pure and evident. My name is Ian, and I am a social worker, this paper addresses the subject of intellectualising social work and anti-oppressive practice.

Sigmund Freud was interested in understanding the human mind in terms of its functions, processes, and conflicts (Almaas, 2000). Mahler, et al, (1975) argued that according to the concept of ego psychology 'the conception of self' is not something one is born with, but something that is socially constructed. Thus, it is a conditioned response to external demands. Identity is a multifaceted human phenomenon (Autiero, 2017). The journey to self has been an essential component for my personal development and social work education in the face of my own adversity. Understanding my own personal responses to people, situations and institutions has been a key aspect of anti-oppressive practice. Dismantling the architectures of my personal rhetoric through the examination of my thinking and behaviour over the period of my life, has allowed me to identify and unearth the deep-rooted belief systems I had developed. My early childhood experiences were the conditions where I cognitively structuralised of a subjective 'blueprint' to the way the world works, which, I translated the way I perceived myself and the world in which I lived in. I have learned that my belief system is the engine that drives my thinking and behaviour. The cognitive processes derived from my egoic projections of separateness and individualism constrained me, when I project, I reject myself, because I deny myself 'real' connection. The truth is I was running from a deep sense of sadness that felt so inconsolable, to feel this was to not survive. The purpose of this paper is to share how I have come to understand that anti-oppressive practice is not just an intellectual activity, we must place more emphasis on human emotional responses to one another. Here lies my own personal insights based on inductive reasoning, where I have drawn a conclusion from a set of specific observations. I recognise that the validity of such can be brought into question, and for the integrity of the points raised it most definitely should be! An honest personal enquiry is what I am to inspire within each reader. I will illustrate my own experiences of coming to be awakened (as I shall call it for the purposes of this paper), I am choosing to be courageous and 'show up' in the glory of my own vulnerabilities, for which I have learned is a key characteristic of legitimate, and authentic connection. I have come to recognise that the beginning of being awakened is to realise that we are subjective beings looking at the world through our own subjective lenses, for those of us who are most honest would realise that we have claimed objectivity within social contexts. If we are all projecting our lives onto one another can there ever be a static social truth? Or is this all based on individual interpretations? This is a key learning point, and personal realisation for the reflective, and introspective social work practitioner.

I will start by making an admission of my own journey and participation to oppressive ideologies and practices and how I have come to understand them, which have inspired me to write about this subject. I will then explore the observations I have made in practice that communicate to me there is more work to be done. Finally, I will offer some insights and perspectives from great teachers and thinkers in the realms of humanity and spirituality.

It takes wisdom to see intention, but we are often judged by our actions. As I write this, I am a qualified social worker, but I am also a human being who is guilty of being on a journey. I know I have consciously engaged in racism, sexism and other forms of conscious and unconscious discrimination, which can lead minority groups to be collectively discriminated against, and therefore oppression can take place (Thompson, 2011). I have contributed to people's life chances being less than average due to my own heteronormative and ethnocentric ideologies. Good social work practice requires me to be a reflective practitioner, which mostly involves an intellectual activity. Did I assess all aspects of the situation, how did I apply theory, did I consider human rights, capacity, legislation, power and personal/ professional agency? What would I do next time and so on... Obviously reflection is very helpful; it has become the cornerstone that shapes practitioners learning and professional development. But what about introspection- the examination and observations of one's own mental and emotional processes?

Kolb's Cycle published (1984) before Gibb's cycle, which was developed to enable educators to review their own teaching and ongoing development. Gibbs Cycle develops the experiential learning theory further by relating teaching methods to Kolb's model (Fiechter, 2021). The reflective learning cycle encourages practitioners to explore their feelings, I advocate for this. However, we need more attention to introspection. John Heron (1970) who coined the phenomenology of social encounter concept, criticises the Kolb Cycle for being too narrow and underdeveloped. I believe that the longest journey in the world I will ever take is just eighteen inches - from my head to my heart. Therefore, I must evolve my insights to look beyond intellectualism alone, I have to have a deep and meaningful engagement with myself voyaging within, unearthing my emotional responses to further my personal discovery.

O'Kane and O'Kane (2016) beautifully illustrate that;

"The suffering we experience in life has more to do with our inability to authentically connect than anything else, but we do not explain it to ourselves that way. We prefer to explain our pain with "him or her or this or that": we prefer to keep the explanation outside ourselves."

My inability to connect was largely to do with my own egoic strategies driven by personal beliefs about the world in which I lived in, and everyone in it. I have had to recount early experiences where the structuralising of my own blueprint took place, and 're-experience' my experiences through experiential personal development workshops in order to re-frame and challenge the lies, or as O'Kane and O'Kane (2016) illustrate 'the suspicion of self' (SOS). I hold a strong memory as a child, perhaps one of the first few I have. I was a very small child, and my twin brother is conveying a message of concern, the look in his eyes tell me everything I need to know. Suddenly in the background I can hear shouting, screaming as it draws in to become louder and louder. I become conscious of the external distress, I feel a sense of fear and uncertainty rise within me, I experience an impending kismet of unsafety that starts to permeate my whole being, this was a common sense of self that I lived with as far back as I can emotionally remember.

I find myself sat at the top of the landing, looking down the stairs as my Mother is being punched in the face, I hear her Liverpudlian accent as she screams out "It's alright kids, it's alright kids..." She is clearly in distress and very frightened, I wonder if she is trying to contain the crises by telling me it's alright, or is this behaviour 'alright'? A short while after, the man that attacks my mother looked up the stairs to see me sat there watching, we make eye contact for a moment, as he looks directly into my eyes as he says; "I love you, Ian." It was here that I learnt some clear messages about the world, this was the construction of my own personal blueprint that became the lens which I saw the world through, the architecture of this blueprint were the values and belief systems that I inherited from my family, which were the driving force behind all my personal thinking, and thus behaviour.

What did I learn about life and the world in which I lived in? I learnt to believe that I was not lovable, because it was not safe to love someone like me. Loving me meant my Mum got hurt. I learnt to believe that this must mean people should not love me, and that was because I was not worthy of love. I learnt to believe that it was ok for me to suffer, so I made myself suffer. I learnt that men were bad, and women were helpless. I was a man; therefore, I am bad. The egoic strategies I adopted to protect myself of the version of love I believed to be true drove me to the brink of insanity. Because I had developed a set of psychological constructs (beliefs) as a result of my experiences. For much of which served me well, I was able to dwell in a perceived sense of safety through not only not connecting but disconnecting through destruction. Self-destruction was the main driving force that overpowered anything that was important to me. I trudged my way through the trenches of self-degradation and self-loathing. Twenty foster homes, three children's homes, thirty-five arrests, six prison sentences, street homeless and intravenous crack and heroin addiction... I abandoned the human being within me. I sold my dignity, my hope and gave up on anything that was important to me, constantly finding reasons to confirm the self-debilitating and destructive belief systems I had made up about myself, or my 'SOS'.

The purpose of this paper is not to provide a holistic in-depth analysis of the internal and external factors of the trauma I experienced and the details of the journey, although that could be a helpful read for some professional insights perhaps. I share this for four reasons; One: I hope that I can speak with some authority when I share from the perspective of the journey I have been on. Two: I have failed, I have hurt people to the point where their lives will never fully recover, the damage I have caused will never be 'undone', I do not speak from an 'ethically right' platform. Three: My self-destructive behaviour has forced me into submission, I have had to undergo a deep and meaningful engagement with myself. Here lies a terrible gift for me. I get to walk the road less travelled, but God knows I have paid the price for it. Four: Finally, I have come to realise there is no static accomplishment, I must keep going and I desperately need people on this journey with me because I cannot do it alone or survive in a world that does not seek legitimate connection. Regardless of what my ego tells me.

I will now fast-forward the tape to when I am thirty years old, and I find myself sat in a social work lecture listening to the work of Neil Thompson (2016) being delivered by a university lecturer. I feel so very lucky to have attended the university I did, there was a clear message that all the lecturers were very passionate about social work. I could see that they genuinely wanted to contribute to our development and professional thinking for the cause of humanity and social work development. By this point in my life, I had worked within the UK Foster Care sector for a good number of years in casual, regional and national roles with some international experience too, working in countries such as Russia, Japan, Canada, Finland and Netherlands to name a few. Although I had heard a previous manager talk a lot about inclusivity, to my surprise I started to realise that I had never heard anyone talk about discrimination and oppression before. Anti-oppressive practice was not something anyone had talked to me about, yet this was such a fundamental aspect of social work thinking and practice. Now I must recognise this could be in part consequential to what I was conscious of, sometimes when a friend drives a new car, you then see that car everywhere. Otherwise known as the Baader-Meinhof phenomenon, or the frequency illusion. Of course, it seems to be everywhere because you're noticing it more. The term "frequency illusion" originated by Stanford linguistics professor Arnold Zwicky in 2005. He also took note of its cousin the recency illusion — "the belief that things YOU have noticed only recently are in fact recent," (Denison, 2018). I think this is also a great critique for the limitations of inductive reasoning as a research method alone, which I have already alluded to.

So, has anti-oppressive practice thinking just appeared, or have I only just become conscious of its existence? Perhaps both. However, it was not a company agenda or a key aspect of team meetings and supervisions I was a part of. To be controversial, I did perceive issues of power and discrimination where foster carers were only committed to looking after 'certain types of children'. This was rarely challenged, which I started to question. The commercialisation of foster care made foster parents a commodity, which can be dehumanising for them. This can be the incubator for a host of challenges that can deny the personal and professional development of foster parents through the fear of upsetting the carer retention strategies, and in turn supports the status quo of ongoing oppression that looked after children can be subjected to. I think a whole paper could be written on this subject alone. But I remain of the position that foster parents are required to do extraordinary work and deserve all the help and support they need to care for our children. I was continually inspired by their tenacity to the children many of them cared for, but we must take note from historical advocators on such issues, for example Gandhi said we must talk about inequality and oppression for it to be changed (Mander, 2015). Interestingly Ghandi, for the majority has historically been an unquestioned figure within mainstream narratives, but if we take a closer look there is an over-reliance on Gandhi's own interpretations of his life, including his autobiographical texts (Roy, 2018). Or for the sake of this paper, his own personal 'blueprint'. African academics; Ashwin Desai and Goolam Vahed spent seven years exploring the complex story of Gandhi who lived in their country for more than two decades - 1893 to 1914. Their book *The South African Gandhi: Stretcher-Bearer of Empire*, challenges the conventional Indian historiography of Gandhi. Their research uncovered Gandhi's private letters and a trail of literature providing evidence that tells a story beyond his own 'intellectual public presentation'. They claim that Gandhi supported more taxes on impoverished African people and turned a blind eye to the brutality of the Empire on Africans, there are others who claim that Gandhi was a colonised elite who supported the British empire (Skaria, 2020; Gerits, 2017; Ashwin, and Goolem, 2015; Modiri, 2019). The point I am making here is that even Mahatma Gandhi a globally acclaimed Indian lawyer, anti-colonial nationalist and political ethicist has written personal letters using derogatory language about the African Black community during in his time in South Africa! Although the claims about his limited views on Black Africans were unsophisticated, even his intellectualism could not save him. I claim in this moment that he had lost sight of his own humanity; he was eighteen inches away from the point. Anti-Oppressive practice is not an intellectual activity.

We would be hard pushed to find a historical influential figure that was good to all people at all times. I have alluded to the work of Sigmund Freud, an Austrian neurologist and the founder of psychoanalysis. There are reasons to believe that engrained Victorian belief systems supported the status quo of sexual abuse that young girls and women were sadly subjected to. Perhaps Freud's Victorian value system or patriarchal 'blueprint' allowed him to legitimise some of his deleterious theories, which today would be considered a serious child protection concern. Early in Freud's career young female patients were sent to him due to a perceived issue of 'hysteria', a common Victorian 'condition' experienced by many women. Symptoms included loss of voice, appetite and compulsive vomiting to name just a few (Freud, 1966; Breuer, 1895). Over a period of time Freud found that the young girls were repeatedly talking about being sexually abused, mainly by their fathers. Freud theorised this as 'Seduction Theory', pointing to a direct relationship to sexual abuse and adult hysteria, which would now be recognised as a deeply distressing trauma response. In a time of Victorian morality underpinned by values of charity, family, duty and sexual propriety, one could imagine that such a reality made Freud feel uneasy. This led him to change his theory, as he stated;

> "*Almost all women patients told me that they had been seduced by their father, I was driven to recognise in the end that these reports were untrue and so came to understand that the hysterical symptoms are derived from phantasies and not from real occurrences.*" (Freud, 1966).

Furthermore, Freud reduced their accounts to an 'imagined' female problem, claiming the women had sexual fantasies of being seduced by their fathers. He coined the 'Oedipus Complex' theory, concluding that these fantasies are derived from a desire for sexual involvement with the parent of the opposite sex (Britton, et al. 1989; Freud, 1924). For a more

ESSAYS

comprehensive examination, see a book by Florence Rush (1980) Best Kept Secret - Sexual Abuse of Children. Here lies a strong argument that some of Freud's theories were neglectful and oppressive towards women in particular. Here also lies an example that exposes the harm of cultural belief systems, the engines which can drive oppression, and can even be inherited by the founder of psychoanalysis. Perhaps Sigmund Freud set out on an intellectual expedition to understand the human mind only to miss the point; human life cannot be fully realised through intellectual means alone. Was he eighteen inches away from the point, would he have done more had he transcended macro ideologies and accessed something deeper within? Anti-Oppressive practice is not an intellectual activity.

I have carved a career out of my own adversity which has landed me on some popular platforms such as the BBC Victoria Derbyshire show, TED X, and working with various international organisations. I have met and spoken with social care practitioners all over the world. I consider myself fortunate in that I feel comfortable to share who I am and the challenges I live with, I have had to learn to embrace and stand in my truth. I have had many private conversations with practitioners who share their personal experiences with me. I have come to realise that social workers often feel drawn to the caring profession because it resonates with something of their own personal experiences. Themes that often emerge through such conversations are issues with addiction, co-dependency, childhood abuse and domestic violence (DV) and having grown up in alternative care. There is often a sense that their experiences should be kept a secret as to maintain their professionalism. I have seen human suffering within the very workforce appointed to respond to social problems/ challenges within our society. I see people sending their own 'representative' in the name of professionalism. I see professional rhetoric as the veil of misuse of power driven by deep insecurity. The level of consciousness social care can operate on will happily countersign this. Like a rich man being congratulated by the neoliberal world, but inside he feels emotionally bankrupt, why? Because getting it right for external causes is not the point of human life. We seek meaning through illegitimate connection, only to end up amplifying our loneliness and despair, so we seek more pleasure, success, money, do another assessment, write another court report and meet KPIs to be congratulated by our manager, surely now we must have self-worth and meaning?

On my second placement I was learning practice in a children's safeguarding team. My practice manager told me that the only way to do this job was to emotionally 'switch off', she advised that I do the same. I was professionally advised to be disconnected. My first case was of a pregnant woman in her third trimester. Due to the risk and vulnerability, I met with the team manager and head of service, they were openly agreeing that the local authority should have the power to force women to be sterilised, and this would be the most effective solution. I was waiting for someone to laugh, because this had to be a joke. No one laughed, they agreed and decided the baby was going to be removed and the unborn assessment was just a proceduralisation. This communicated to me that they believed people were incapable of change, and a draconian response prevailed human rights. I could not help but consider that if their philosophy on how to respond to human suffering were common practice I could not have been born, because I was not my mother's first child. I spent some time in the child protection team mostly responding to Section 47 and 17 (Children Act, 1989). I was talking with two female practitioners who shared that they 'love to work on domestic violent cases', this was due to their own experiences of being victims of DV, this somehow made them feel empowered. I believe that there are many reasons for this type of culture, and in truth I can only speculate as I cannot speak for the individuals I reference. I believe this is a strategic self's fear-based projection, they seek resolution through helping other women, this is not inherently bad, but is vulnerable to issues of power, transference and oppressive practice if looking through the lens of one's own trauma. Paradoxically, here lies the potential for a powerful connection through intersubjectivity- the sharing of subjective experience between two or more people. Relationships based on identification can cultivate trust and offer opportunity for healing. So many social workers are 'experts by experience' and perhaps more thought should be given to this. What could be achieved if we were more open about our trauma? Rumi famously said, 'The wound is the place where the light enters you' (Udoyono, 2021).

Day in and day out the social workers I speak of face trauma that may well resonate with their own experiences, we should also not rule out the impact of secondary trauma. They all had procedural and educational insights, but they were eighteen inches away from the real point of it all, their emotional sphere. The less we are willing to feel, the more we develop finely attuned strategies and defences that prevent us from healing the wounds we otherwise seek to amend in areas that cause more disconnection and rob us of the innocence we can see in people, even those that have harmed us. Anti-oppressive practice is not an intellectual activity alone, we are required to have a deep and meaningful engagement with ourselves. We do not become disconnected because of these issues; we have these issues because we have become disconnected. Relationship based practice is more than a rhetoric, that worryingly is being highjacked by bureaucracy and proceduralisation. The harm I experienced was done in relationship, the healing has also taken place in relationship too. I must 'show up' and be vulnerable, here I can be 'seen', the men that tell me they love me today do not hit my mother, or any other women. They do not harm me, but I had to seek relationships that were willing to journey with me so I could re-frame my view. Seeking men who abused women and children in my social work role was never the answer, such an approach would be deleterious for me and anyone I seek to help. I would be looking to reconfirm the negative messages I hold about men, again and again, while I continue to feel a secret sense of shame for being a man. We have to risk allowing ourselves to be seen, in all our vulnerably. It took me so much longer to realise that I used people like I used drugs, I even used people in the pursuit of trying to fix my trauma within my professional capacity! I have to be willing to challenge my own fears, rather than letting those fears drive my professional and personal decision-making in life. There is a wonderful line in The Tibetan book of living and dying; "The more we try to run away from that fear, the more monstrous it becomes." (Sogyal, 2008).

I have come to know truth as emotional honesty, here I find that we are all more alike than different, our drivers, needs and insecurities speak of an experience that I believe is a manifestation of divine spirit. Love is the antidote to human conflict, here I am reminded of Rumi "Your task is not to seek for love, but merely to seek and find all the barriers within yourself that you have built against it." (Robinson, 2016). To me, recovery starts with a deep and meaningful engagement with self. It is here I address my barriers to love. The early beginnings of my life were the breeding place for a lifelong consequence that have required me to undertake a journey of recovery. To quote Gabor Maté (2008) *"The greatest damage done by neglect, trauma or emotional loss is not the immediate pain they inflict but the long-term distortions they induce in the way a developing child will continue to interpret the world and her situation in it."* I recognise that trauma will be passed on and carried down until someone is ready and willing to feel it, our future children depend on us to feel and authentically connect. For me personally, there is a philosophical and spiritual aspect to anti-oppressive practice. A senior member of a 12-step recovery group once said; "We must learn to suffer and find God." Now I recognise that this may appear morbid, but can we truly live a life absent of suffering? We must learn to be with our pain. It has been said that the fastest way to get to hell is to try and run from hell, and to quote Gabor Maté; *"The road to hell is not paved with good intentions. It is paved with lack of intention."* With this insight we now stand at a crossroads, we all live to a 'program' of living, either a conscious one or an unconscious one. We now have enough consciousness to make a decision, do we grow as spiritual beings realising ourselves through this human experience? As for the God part, I believe that there is a reality beyond the animalistic five senses, in meditative state and conscious connected breath work I have accessed inner states that I believe are connected to a universal vibration of an existence underlying the totality of all reality. Here I have transcended ego and found an inner truth of love and peace.

The French philosopher, Pierre Teilhard de Chardin said; *"We are not human beings having a spiritual experience. We are spiritual beings having a human experience."* Spirituality is an under discussed topic in social work. When we transcend to broader universal perspectives more can be understood, perhaps there is a deeper meaning beyond our limited conceptualisation of life as we know it, with this perspective can we be more optimistic, accepting of ourselves and one another. I lean on the work of Deepak Chopra (2007) for an in-depth analysis of material reality- the world of objects and events is really Quantum reality, which is just a transition zone where energy turns into matter. We are manifestations of this energy; I believe more can be healed and understood through it. We can sometimes see the world through very limited human judgment, 'good', 'bad', 'right' or 'wrong'. As I have already referenced the work of Rumi who was deeply spiritual and a luminary of his time, who continues to expand human consciousness through his poetry as he wrote, "*Out beyond ideas of wrongdoing and right doing, there is a field. I'll meet you there.*" Perhaps this is a paradigm that can lead us to real inclusivity from a universal perspective, and thus anti-oppressive practice.

In the context of why we are all here I love you! Because my life has changed because of love, and now my life depends on love, and I believe that social work depends on love too! This is why anti-oppressive practice is so much more than an intellectual activity. The survival of our humanitarian global community does in fact depend on love. Language is the adhesive that binds culture, let emotional truth be the currency of all our communication.

With love, Ian Thomas.

ESSAYS

Autiero, G. (2017) Ethnic identity and scholastic effort: a multifaceted approach IZA Journal of Development and Migration, vol. 7, no. 1, pp. 1-13. Available at: https://search-proquest-com. ezproxy.bcu.ac.uk/docview/2073234674?pq-origsite=summon

Ashwin, D., Goolem, V. (2015) The South African Gandhi: Stretcher-Bearer of Empire (South Asia in Motion). Stanford University Press.

Almaas, A.H. (2000) The void: Inner spaciousness and ego structure. Shambhala Publications.

Burton, A., Devji, F., Sinha, M., Soske, J., Desai, A. and Vahed, G. (2018) *The South African Gandhi: Stretcher-Bearer of Empire.* Journal of Natal and Zulu History, 32(1), pp.100-118.

Britton, R., Feldman, M. and O'Shaughnessy, E. (1989) The Oedipus complex today. London: Karnac.

Chopra, D. (2007) How to know god: The soul's journey into the mystery of mysteries. Harmony.

Denison, D.(2018) That-clauses as complements of verbs or nouns. In Subordination in English (pp. 61-84). De Gruyter Mouton. Fiechter, K.,2021. Differences Between Gibbs and Kolb Cycles. Science & education.

Freud, S., (1966) with Breuer, J. (1895) Studies on Hysteria. J. Strachey (Ed. and Trans.), The standard edition of the complete psychological works of Sigmund Freud, 2, pp.1953-1974.

Freud, S.1924) The passing of the Oedipus complex. International journal of psycho-analysis, 5, pp.419-424.Available at: https://pep-web.org/browse/document/ijp.005.0419a?page=P0419

Gerits, F. (2017) The South African Gandhi: stretcher-bearer of empire.

Heron, J. (1970) The phenomenology of social encounter: The gaze. Philosophy and Phenomenological Research, 31(2), pp.243-264.

Heron, J. (1992) Feeling and personhood: Psychology in another key. Sage.

Mahler, M.S., Pine, F. and Bergman, A. (1975) The psychological birth of the child. New York: Basic.

Mander, H.(2015) Looking away: inequality, prejudice and indifference in new India. New Delhi: Speaking Tiger.

Maté, G.(2008) In the realm of hungry ghosts: Close encounters with addiction. Random House Digital, Inc.

Modiri, J.M. (2019) Race, history, irresolution: Reflections on City of Tshwane Metropolitan Municipality v Afriforum and the limits of" post"-apartheid constitutionalism. De Jure Law Journal, 52(1), pp.27-46. Available at: http://www.scielo.org.za/scielo.php?script=sci_arttext&pid=S2225-71602019000100002

O'Kane, C. and O'Kane, D. REAL. Clearmind Publishing. Kindle Edition.

Robinson, J. (2016) On Depressive Realism and humanistic therapy. Self & Society, 44(4), pp.468-469.

Rush, F. (1980) The best kept secret: Sexual abuse of children (p. 98). Englewood Cliffs, NJ: Prentice-Hall.

Rush, F. (1996) The Freudian coverup. Feminism & Psychology, 6(2), pp.260-276. Available at: https://journals.sagepub.com/doi/abs/10.1177/0959353596062015?journalCode=fapa

Roy, P.(2018) Ashwin Desai and Goolam Vahed. The South African Gandhi: Stretcher-Bearer of Empire. South Asia in Motion. Stanford: Stanford University Press, 2016. Pp. 343. $24.95. Journal of British Studies, 57(1), pp.192-193.

Sogyal, R. (2008) The Tibetan book of living and dying. Random House.

Skaria, A. (2020). Thinking with Gandhi on racism and violence: A letter to a friend. ABC Religion and ethics. Available at: https://www.abc.net.au/religion/thinking-with-gandhi-on-racism-and-violence/12424422

Steiner, J. (1985) Turning a blind eye: The cover up for Oedipus. International review of psycho-analysis, 12, pp.161-172. Available at: https://pep-web.org/browse/document/IRP.012.0161A

Smith, D. L. (2013). Beyond good and evil: Variations on some Freudian themes. In A. C. Bohart, B. S. Held, E. Mendelowitz, & K. J. Schneider (Eds.), Humanity's dark side: Evil, destructive experience, and psychotherapy (pp. 193–212). American Psychological Association. https://doi.org/10.1037/13941-010

Thompson, N. (2011) Promoting Equality. (Third Edition) London: Palgrave.

Thompson, N. (2016) Anti-Discriminatory Practice. (Sixth edition) London: Palgrave.

Udoyono, B. (2021) Fix Your Life with the Wisdom of Rumi. Bambang Udoyono.

Why we need the Association of Care Experienced Social Care Workers

- Dr Trevor Rodgers-Gray

There is a large and growing body of literature that explores and attempts to understand the experiences and outcomes of care leavers, particularly those who have recently left the care system (see Goddard *et al.*, 2008, and Harrison *et al.*, 2020, for example). In the UK there are over 80,000 children and young people looked after by the state with almost 30,000 leaving care (DfE, 2021). Of these people leaving care many go on to train and practise in social care, including as social workers. A new (June 2021) national association of care-experienced social care workers (ACESCW) was formed to support this group of people.

Care-experienced social workers work alongside social work colleagues carrying out all the duties that constitute social work. However, their care-experience is often unknown to their colleagues, and thus is a hidden aspect of their identity. Indeed, care-experienced practitioners are not seen as a definite group, and so their care-heritage may be better understood as a hidden, second identity. There are parallels here with the thesis of Sedgwick (1990) who argues that since there are no external cues to identify gay and lesbian people, (it is a hidden aspect of their identity, as is care-heritage), if they choose to 'come out' they must do so actively and with every new social encounter. Sedgewick thus argues that identifying as gay or lesbian is a specific and unique experience not shared in any other identification. Care-experienced social workers as an identity group may share this experience of specificity.

Care-experienced social workers have at times, felt ashamed, anxious, and angry about their pre-social work experience (Newcomb *et al.*, 2017, Dickson, 2021). Indeed, care experienced social work practitioners experience discrimination. For example, some care-experienced social work practitioners have said that some social work colleagues treat them as different, less professional, less trustworthy, or even more vulnerable for no reason other than their care experience (Dickson, 2021).

Care-experienced social workers straddle the divide between social work practitioners and those they serve (children and families that use social services), including the potentially conflicting internal roles that may be experienced (Newcomb *et al.*, 2017). Indeed, some care experienced social workers find that their own families or people they have grown up with treat them with suspicion as though they have somehow betrayed their own kind and joined the opposition. Care experienced social workers are sometimes told not to discuss their own care backgrounds with the people they work with. Moreover, they may have to address triggering emotions in themselves as they carry out their work but ensure the impact of emotionality on a professional role is limited and appropriate.

Social workers work with the most disadvantaged and marginalised people within society (BASW, 2021). Care-experienced social workers are therefore an important group of the social work profession for several reasons that are outlined here: Firstly, their care-heritage gives them insights into the experience and process of receiving statutory care as children (insider knowledge). Secondly, children and young people who receive statutory care are disproportionately from minority or otherwise oppressed identity groups that experience discrimination and disadvantage, for example black and other ethnic minorities, working class families and

ESSAYS

communities, (see Harrison, 2020, and Hammond, 2020, for example). It is likely therefore that care-experienced social workers have experienced similar forms of discrimination based on class, race etc., and as such this too suggests that care-experienced social workers working with children, will have shared experiences with those they support as professionals. Moreover, as a minority group within the social work profession, care-experienced social workers experience 'minority stress' because of social disadvantage, prejudice, and discrimination (Meyer, 2003). The ACESCW therefore, represents a fantastic opportunity to support and learn from care experienced practitioners, and in turn, to support people in receipt of social work services.

British Association for Social Workers (BASW) (2021) What do social workers do? (basw.co.uk) Accessed 25th July 2021

Department for Education (DfE) (2021) Children looked after in England including adoptions, Reporting Year 2020 – Explore education statistics – GOV.UK (explore-education-statistics. service.gov.uk) Accessed 12th July 2021

Dickson, I. (2021) Stigma of Care felt by those in our profession. Professional Social Worker

Goddard, J. & Feast, J. & Kirton, D. (2008) A Childhood on Paper: Managing Access to Child Care Files by Post-Care Adults. Adoption & Fostering Journal. 32. 50-62.

Hammond, S., Young, J., & Duddy, C. (2020) Life Story Work with Children and Young People with Care Experience: A Scoping review. Developmental Child Welfare. 2(4), 293-315.

Harrison, N., Baker, Z., & Stevenson, J. (2020) 'Employment and further study outcomes for care-experienced graduates in the UK', Higher education, pp. 1–22.

Harrison, N. (2020) Patterns of participation in higher education for care-experienced students in England: why has there not been more progress?, Studies in Higher Education, 45:9, 1986-2000.

Meyer I. H. (2003) Prejudice, social stress, and mental health in lesbian, gay, and bisexual populations: conceptual issues and research evidence. Psychological bulletin, 129(5), 674–697.

Newcomb, M. Burton, J., & Edwards, N. (2017) Service User or Service Provider? How Social Work and Human Services Students Integrate Dual Identities. Social Work Education, 36(6), 678-689.

Sedgwick, E. K. (1990) Epistemology of the Closet. California: University of California Press.

ESSAYS

The Association of Care Experienced Social Care Workers

- Dr Janet Melville-Wiseman and Dr Trevor Rodgers-Gray

"Leave no stone unturned to ensure the profession learns
from failings of the past"

(ACESCW Manifesto 2021)

Introduction

The Association of Care Experienced Social Care Workers (ACESCW) was formed in June 2021. It was the original idea of Ian Dickson following the highly successful and influential Care Experienced Conference in 2019. Although Ian has now delegated the development of ACESCW we are immensely grateful for his pioneering work that has led us to where we are today. It is a national organisation made up of a diverse group of people with different outlooks, perspectives, and priorities, but all of whom have the shared experience of care as children and young people. However, we are all now practising within social work or social care (as social workers, social care workers and providers, managers, students, and academics) or are recently retired from those roles.

This chapter presents a collation of the thoughts, views and experiences of ACESCW's inaugural members about the organisation and why it is needed.

It is difficult for us to articulate the significance of the ACESCW personally, and perhaps more so, its value to others. The reasons for this are multifaceted, although a key explanation is that there was no 'space' where we could be open and share who we are. With the formation of ACESCW that space was created. The ACESCW provides a new experience of 'care' – care for those with shared heritage as children and young people, care for the impact of profound and painful journeys undertaken however recent or distant, and care to create a new environment for those yet to become care experienced social care workers. As with the most effective and influential values-based organisations it has developed from the bottom up by people with lived experiences of care and who know why things need to be challenged and changed.

This essay has given us an opportunity to answer two important questions. What is the value of ACESCW to us or to others? and how can ACESCW support, influence and perhaps challenge social work and social work education? Contributors have chosen whether to be identified by their full name, first name, or a pseudonym and this reflects one of the shared experiences of enduring stigma in relation to being care experienced. The group are collectively pioneers to challenge and change this stigma. In addition, we present the ACESCW's manifesto developed by Ian Dickson and others in the first days of ACESCW.

What is the value of ACESCW to you or others?

To address this question, it is necessary to reflect on our experiences prior to the formation of the ACESCW. Whilst we are a diverse group, there are some experiences that are common to many of us.

> "We all relate to the same emotional turmoil and experiences of oppression by being looked after by the state and then being on the other end of support." (**Mary Carter**)

However, our experiences in relation to our places of work have not always reflected the value that our earlier experiences bring and have often been very difficult. Some examples reflect an erroneous assumption that in spite of being fully qualified, we may not be up to the job with:

> "...accusations of being 'too close', 'too involved', 'not having the distance needed', and other such phrases." (**David Anderson**)

Such experiences, mean that many care experienced social workers have hidden, and continue to hide, their care-heritage.

> "I've never shared with anyone at work my care experienced past because I feared judgement and 'reduction' to only that side of me." (**Karin Heber**)

This is echoed by, Marie:

> "I have never been able to discuss the dichotomy of being care experienced and working in social care. I often found myself wondering where I fitted. It was like I needed to choose a team. I am either a professional who has succeeded or the care experienced person who will never be professional enough." (**Marie**)

This naturally leads to a lack of authenticity and feelings of shame. As Annette painfully recounts:

> "[the] repeated lies about a fundamental part of my identity made me feel shameful."

She goes on to say,

> "I felt conflicted between allowing the gift of empathy to shine a light onto the path that I was walking with families, honouring how my own story could help others to start to make sense of theirs, [versus] the value of having a sense of belonging in the workplace." (**Annette Frewin**)

A deep need to belong and a safe space to call 'home' is another theme common to many of us. As Kyla, says,

> "*I was living in the borderlands, that space where you have one foot in and out - yet don't seem to sit anywhere.*" (**Kyla**)

The longing is expressed clearly by, Annette:

> "*I was thirsty for a deeper connection with other social workers who had been through the care system.*" (**Annette Frewin**)

The value of the ACESCW cannot be overstated in terms of being accepted for who you are, to "*listen and feel heard*", (Mike S.), and to have a safe space:

> "*...where friendships will form...to sit in both the world of care experienced and working in social care...where both worlds intertwine.*" (**Marie**).

As Karin shares:

> "*I find it very refreshing to be able to share my experience with fellow social workers. It feels good to be open, honest, and accepted/not judged at our meetings. It validates my beliefs.*" (**Karin Heber**)

However, it is not the only motivation of the ACESCW. Our care experience means, "*...we all bring powerful and monumental insight to the profession.*" (**Mary Carter**)

As David Anderson notes, the song lyric, "*Come from the Shadows*" captures the bottom-up emergence of our Association. Indeed,

> "*...there has been a passionate and strenuous effort to reclaim the narrative by people who have experienced care.*" (**David Anderson**)

Thus, we are, *"in position where we feel ready to speak up, challenge and educate the profession."* (**Mary Carter**)

How can ACESCW support, influence and perhaps challenge social work and social work education?

It would be unacceptable to make pejorative judgements about a doctor and their ability to practice if they had experienced serious physical or mental health problems before their training, during their training or during their practice – in fact it would be outlawed in the UK by the Equality Act 2010. However, the law does not yet provide the same protection for Care Experienced people when they become social care and social work practitioners. One aim of the ACESCW is to challenge this situation and the underlying stigma that currently exists. In doing so we remember that Care Experienced people did not chose the life they had to lead and if some welcomed the opportunity to be in care it was because there was no better alternative. We also did not choose the system that provided that care and which often exacerbated our original traumatic experiences. However, we have chosen our careers and provide unique perspectives which are not to be stigmatised or used to make us lesser professionals. Annette describes a training session she delivered on the use of life story work and included some of her own:

> *"After the presentation, I was praised for my bravery in sharing my own life story book with the team, but in my head, I questioned, why shouldn't I and why am I being looked at with faces of sympathy, shouldn't we all feel that sense of empowerment to share our stories as these are what make us who we are and they aren't to be ashamed of."* (**Annette Frewin**)

Hannah shared the unique connectedness we have with the people we work with and how that is not always valued:

"Care experienced social workers have lived through much of the adversity affecting families today and have a great deal of knowledge and wisdom from this which enables us to positively contribute to the lives of those we support. Sadly, not all professionals can recognise the strength of having care experienced social workers in practice and we sometimes face stigmatisation, both consciously and unconsciously." (**Hannah Ide**)

Marie highlights the personal impact of these experiences of what is inherent stigma and prejudice towards us:

"I am yet to attend an ACESCW meeting where there is not discussion regarding unfair judgment of someone who is care experienced whilst at work. I am yet to sit through a meeting where someone hasn't been judged or treated different because they are care experienced. It is hard to hear that the people we work amongst can struggle to accept our histories." (**Marie**)

It is sometimes difficult to comprehend the reasoning behind these attitudes or where allies might be found. Annette described an all too familiar management response:

"One of my colleagues shared with me that I needed to be careful at work as they were aware that management had been questioning whether some of my emotional responses were provoked due to me growing up in care; I was so disheartened to hear that..."(**Annette Frewin**)

Challenging such stigma can be impossible in isolation which is why supporting each other, and challenging stigma collectively is a core aim of ACESCW. Our membership is already over 70 and is likely to increase substantially. So instead of stigma we would like our experiences to be a source of celebration and positive regard:

"When will our care experience status be celebrated instead of being a barrier? I want people to understand that care experienced people don't stop becoming care experienced once our files closed. I am senior social worker now and the importance of my care experience has not lessened. My care experience is a large part of my identity and that is still the case 15 years on." (**Marie**)

ACESCW can also bring unique insights into how providers of services, lecturers and researchers should work alongside service users in a collaborative and connected way:

"The best social work in my opinion is co-produced and promotes connection between service user and service giver - ACESCW is all about the grey area, the void in between service user and service giver: the place which could change how practice looks, the place where practice is reflexive and reflective." (**Mike. S**)

Here Karin cautions against the incongruous 'othering' of us in spite of training and the imperative to do the opposite:

"...despite our expected anti-oppression values we continue to "other" service users. We 'normal' social workers against 'vulnerable/care experienced/disabled/ disadvantaged...' service users whilst ignoring the fact that we are all human beings who may require or benefit from support at different stages in our lives. Hence "experts by experience" are never social workers with experience of e.g. care, addiction, prison etc." (**Karin Heber**)

The establishment of ACESCW also provides us with an opportunity to influence policy and practice as key stakeholders in different debates and for those developing policy to draw on our rich and unique perspectives. This will be a key part of our work recognising that urgent changes are unlikely to happen without us representing our perspectives to those who have the power to change things:

> *"Despite me challenging the use of the term 'LAC' and 'CIN' in the local authority: how are children, young people and families 'lacking' and doesn't the acronym of 'CIN' automatically portray people in a negative light? The response I was given to this was 'this is how it is; we can't change it; we can only do our part as individuals as we are responsible for our own practice and we do not speak these terms in front of families'."* (**Annette Frewin**)

We would also wish to support Care Experienced students or newly qualified workers through a buddying or mentoring scheme and will be looking into how this might be facilitated. We will also be looking at how we can provide input into education and to act as consultants to other organisations who are committed to an inclusive approach to care experienced professionals.

Kyla states her hope that ACESCW can:

> *"...provide over site of any policy/guidance relating to care experienced students and practice. I feel it's vital to use lived experience to push for change and work to improve systems for children and families at all levels."* (**Kyla**)

So, finally, what is the value of the ACESCW? Put simply, the *"ACEWSC is at the beating heart of the care experienced community."* (**Mary Carter**)

We are here and will support each other:

> *"Peer support and empowerment are so valuable to me, and I am grateful to have this as I grapple with some of the challenges and rewards that being a care experienced practitioner brings."* (**Kyla**)

"I am in awe of the lives we are all living, despite challenges. We have friendships, bring up children, have fun, have loving relationships and contribute towards a better world. I want to celebrate that. I want our voices and experiences to be heard instead of being hidden by shame and secrecy. I want professionals to come alongside us and celebrate with us. I want them to embrace our care experience." (**Marie**)

"We have come to realise that our own individual feelings are not isolated, and we are not alone." (**Mary Carter**)

"...being able to reach out to other care experienced social workers and hear how much they've achieved is truly empowering." (**Hannah Ide**)

"We don't want others to go through what we were forced to go through, or we want others to experience the love and care we experienced (or both)." (**David Anderson**)

We are, *"happy that ACESCW has formed, and [we're] excited for the journey ahead!"* (**Hannah Ide**)

This chapter invites allies to support us with this essential initiative and for care experienced people in our professions to find a safe space:

"My hope is that by us joining as a group to share some of our experiences with you, hearing and seeing these stories will help you to discover that the silent stigmatisation is not your isolated experience, so it is important to fearlessly challenge any injustice you may encounter or see someone else encountering." (**Annette Frewin**)

If you would like to join us there will never be a requirement to disclose your history but will be welcome to join. As David encapsulates:

"Too many in the professions carry their experience alone, sometimes fearful of being 'found out'. Others – myself included – are at a stage where they choose to share some or all of their story...Our history – whatever it is – can be used as an asset. It is time, time to come from the shadows. ACESCW will be the conduit for that emerging force."
(**David Anderson**)

ACESCW Manifesto

Preface:

The dichotomy of having lived experience of a care system, alongside being an adult representing a profession that provides care, is a complex position to take. We, the members of ACESCW, are familiar with the need for truly relational practice, and recognise the importance of capturing life stories and narratives; being trauma aware and understanding development beyond trauma. Our daily practice includes routine reflection upon our 'use of self', the 'wounded helper', and the significance of constructing and reconstructing meaning.

ACESCW will:

1. Create communities of care, by enabling peer support and mentoring, discussion groups and inquiry

2. Educate, harness empathy and empower, through use of learning materials, resources, consultancy, research, experience and evidence based practice

3. Be proud of our profession, our practice and our journey; which should be protected. We will stand tall and united, be a badge of identity, and raise voices of care experienced people and the profession, challenge the orthodoxy and furthermore lobby and seek to inspire children in care and care leavers.

ACESCW will provide an opportunity to tap into the often unseen potential from extremely proud professionals who have experienced the care system, whereby there is a chance to seriously help others.

Membership

ACESCW will be open to care experienced social workers of all grades and roles, and to all social work students on approved training courses. It will also be open to all those working professionally in social work roles who may not have qualified as social workers.

Management and administration

ACESCW will be managed and administered by an elected Board; elected by the membership. This Board may include:

- A Chair/co-chairs
- A secretary/secretariat
- A treasurer/fund raising lead officer
- A pastoral care/welfare lead officer
- An education/training officer
- A media/press officer

Volunteers from the ACESCW may be invited to stand for office in these lead roles, or to act as team members working as part of sub teams under these leads, to address these specialist areas of interest.

Confidentiality

ACESCW will respect the confidentiality of its members. No lists of members will be placed in the public domain or shared without prior permission of the membership, and correspondence, minutes or information from the

Association will not name or identify individual members so that confidentiality & anonymity can be protected at all times.

Focus of ACESCW

ACESCW will focus on several key areas, in brief:

I. Pastoral care

ACESCW will seek to offer individual and group support to the members. It will be a safe place to be, to gain support and encouragement, advice, a place to vent safely, a place to obtain peer support by 'buddying' and to support wellbeing, for example:

II. Challenging stigma and discrimination

ACESCW will challenge the stigma and discriminatory attitudes displayed towards care experienced social care workers and social work students with government and politicians on their behalf, for example, advocating for care experience to be a 'protected characteristic'.

ACESCW will actively promote the many positive images and unique insights that the care experienced bring to the profession.

Members of ACESCW, with their massive diversity of skills and experiences will offer a forum to share information and advice to its members about issues of interest to them as a group, or between individual members.

III. Political lobbying

ACESCW will represent the interests and cause of care experienced social workers, social work students and social care workers, to politicians, professionals and those making decisions that potentially impact upon the members of the group.

IV. Training

ACESCW will seek to offer training and information about working as a care experienced professional in social care, and the issues and insights that brings and it will consider how best to use them for the good of the members, those we work with, and the profession.

V. Research

ACESCW will seek to support and promote research that promotes insights and learning into the care experienced and working as a care experienced professional in social care.

You feel shame, we should be ashamed

- Anon

I am privileged to be able to write this essay as my story is unique. I am not a 'care leaver,' I was not a 'looked after child,' I was not a 'LAC' or the new term I really don't like 'a previously looked after child.' My story is that I am a social worker who had the fortunate and insightful experience of working with a colleague who was a care leaver.

I wanted to write this essay to highlight the pervasive nature of discrimination and stigma that I witnessed a valued colleague tolerate, which is supported by the fact I write anonymously as I worry what she would have to tolerate if my views of her experiences became known. I chose the word tolerate carefully as originally I wrote suffer but there were back handed compliments directed to her too. Whilst others thought they were complimenting her I watched her tolerate these comments and saw how it added to the shame she already felt. This is my story about Maddie the care leaver.

I currently work for a Local Authority in a team that works with children in care and this is where I met Maddie. When I joined the team we instantly connected, at first I thought it was because we were both newly qualified workers with contemporary social work training. We used to hear phrases thrown across the office such as referring to children and their families as 'cases.' References to 'children being beyond parental control,' and yes I know that is written into the Children Act but it was a term deemed appropriate in 1989! The use of the term 'contact' to describe a child's time with their family and social workers being amazed when children, young people and families got offended. There were many more, and every time we heard them me and Maddie would just look at each other and shake our heads, not quite confident enough to directly challenge what we were hearing, although that time did come.

As I got to know Maddie more, we shared our backgrounds with each other and she told me how she had grown up in care living with a number of foster carers. She had also shared this with other colleagues as well and I began to hear comments of how well Maddie had done bearing in mind she was a care leaver. I heard colleagues tell her to her face that she had done so well 'when the odds were stacked against you.'

These apparently well-meant comments sat uncomfortably with me. Maddie was being labelled and stigmatised as soon as she told people of her lived experiences. Maddie was being identified as a care leaver who had done marvellous things by doing well at school, getting into university, gaining a degree and then being selected to work in this great profession of ours. By sharing her past her professional identity quickly changed in the eyes of her colleagues. She was no longer a social worker but a care leaver all over again.

Maddie was being compared to other young people who have left care and not been as fortunate, she was placed in a group in the minds of her colleagues as someone who had broken the mould. It seems to me that care leavers are not individuals but a collective who are expected to fail because statistically outcomes are different when compared to children who grow up with their birth families (Jackson, 2010; O'Higgins, Sebba and Luke, 2015).

Watching Maddie in practice as a Social Worker was inspiring. She had an ability to quickly connect with children and young people, her desire to maintain important connections to family members and advocate for parents only benefitted those that she worked with. She understood the impact of childhood trauma and she found creative ways of working with children and families. She focussed on reunification, where it was achievable, which quite frankly is never considered by social workers when working with looked after children in my experience. We work in a profession that teaches us to practice in a strengths-based way, to recognise all people have the capacity to make positive changes yet once a child is in care they generally stay there. Maddie was different, she saw potential in people that others did not.

Sadly, Maddie was living a double life, not by choice. One where she could be herself at work and fulfil her ambitions as it was her safe space, but one where outside of work she lived in fear because of an abusive partner. Maddie found the inner strength to tell people about the living nightmare she had endured in her private life and the perpetrator was brought to justice, but not before Maddie's mental health deteriorated leading to a short time off work.

That is when the real discrimination began. Maddie was a care leaver, 'what do you expect?' Maddie was not a frightened victim of domestic abuse but 'a liar who endangered the lives of the children she worked with by not reporting things sooner. We all knew it was happening, but she denied it.' Maddie was living a life where 'history is just repeating itself for her family.' Maddie already felt shame because of her life experiences. I always felt this hard to understand as in simplistic terms Maddie's parents could not keep her safe, so she was placed into care. How did she feel shame? However, as I watched this narrative of Maddie the care leaver developing, I really did get it. Her identity was being etched away from her in her absence. The bright, intelligent, happy, inspiring Maddie was being seen as a sad, stupid liar who didn't walk away from her abusive partner. How was this possible?

As I write these comments I am embarrassed for my profession. One where we understand the impact of domestic abuse, where we understand the strength and bravery needed for someone to take positive action against the perpetrator. How on earth, with our level of training can we seek to suggest a social worker has endangered the life of the children they work with because they were being abused? The answer is easy. It is because Maddie was a care leaver, and the rules are different because nothing other than being a victim was expected of her. Discrimination, blame and labelling at its finest. The shame of her situation being compounded by the shame she already carried like a large weight because of her 'status' as a care leaver. I do not believe that I would be labelled in the same way if I had been Maddie, as I grew up with my parents. I would have got support, attention and much more help than she did. Maddie was alone, a feeling she probably felt for most of her life growing up as she moved between foster placements, separated from her siblings and living a life she felt was her 'normal.'

Mannay et al (2018) view children and young people as being the expert in their own lives. As social workers we listen to children and young people to gain their views and to help them make decisions. Yet many of the children and young people that we work with find this difficult to engage in as they are not in a place where they can make sense of their lived experiences to date or work therapeutically to process the traumatic events they have survived. Yet we have this amazing resource at our disposal, we have social workers who have experience of care, so why do we not hear their voices? I think the answer is that a voice cannot have an impact if no one is listening.

I would like to direct a message to my social work colleagues who have experience of care on behalf of those of us who do not share your insight. We must stop labelling you, we must stop analysing you through a trauma lens, working out whether you are up to the job or too 'damaged' to work with young people. We must stop trying to assess whether you have a secure base of attachment as social workers love to do despite not being psychologists.

Instead, let us tell you that you inspire us, you will be amazing role models for the young people we work with. That you should share your experiences without the threat of being accused of not having appropriate boundaries between you and the young person. Let us recognise you as an expert, someone we should consult routinely to understand the feelings of the young people we work with.

Let us remind you that you matter, that your voices should be loud and heard. Every one of your life experiences matter and have a place in helping the young people we work with.

Maddie inspired me from the day I met her and continues to inspire me now which informs my practice. I remember a conversation with her which she had never considered and the realisation of it created a shift in her thinking. Maddie was not a 'care experienced person,' neither was she a care experienced social worker. Maddie was a social worker with experience of care. Make that same shift in your professional identity as you genuinely matter and belong in social care.

I contacted Maddie once this piece of work had been accepted into this amazing book and asked her to read what I had written. Maddie's view was that I had 'helped us (care leavers) feel heard.' This upset me and I told her that whilst our life experiences are different, the point of my essay was that we are actually the same as we are social workers. Maddie's response was that she did not feel the same and felt like an outsider. Shame really is the most powerful of emotions. So, my final message to Maddie and other social workers with care experience is that professionally we are the same.

Maddie continues to work hard to advocate for children who can no longer live with their families. She uses her experiences to train, mentor and support others. She is also recruiting the next generation of social workers who are care experienced.

I would like to dedicate this piece of work to C, a young care leaver who found life too hard. she will be greatly missed.

Jackson, S. (2010) *Reconnecting care and education: From the Children Act 1989 to care matters.* Journal of Children's Services, 5:3, Pg 48-60. Available online https://doi.org/10. .5042/jcs.2010.0550 (Accessed 15th March 2022)

Mannay, D. Staples, E. Hallet, S. Roberts, L. Rees, A. Evans, R. and Andrews, D. (2018) *Enabling talk and reframing messages: working creatively with care experienced children and young people to recount and re-represent their everyday experiences.* Child in Care Practice, 25:1, Pg 51-63. Available online https://doi.org/10.1080/13575279.201 8.1521375 (Accessed 15th March 2022)

O'Higgins, A. Sebba, J. and Luke, N. (2015) *What is the relationship between being in care and the educational outcomes of children?* Oxford: Rees Centre for Research in Fostering and Education.

The Social Work Student Connect team hosted a webinar with a panel of care experienced students and practitioners, called To Share or Not to Share? in March 2022, just as this book was going to print. If you would like to watch that powerful webinar then use the QR code below.

Don't make a difference..
...be the difference

- Paul Yusuf McCormack

There are lots of good intentions out there and lots of people adhere to them, but good intentions don't make real differences; they don't make the changes that need to happen; they don't sustain and make permanent positive differences.

I wrote this because I have, unfortunately, come across a lot of 'well meaning' people who really want to know about my experiences of life, then sadly they are patronising in their comments and still do what they want to do. This simply proves to me that they don't really hear or understand. Yet these people are the very people who could influence positive change, these are the people who could be the difference.

My message is simply, don't feel sorry for me. You can't change my past; it is what it is. The future however is really where it's at. Let my words be a beginning, let them start the ball rolling and make changes that stick.

Don't make a difference...
...be the difference

If you've really listened to me,
if you really hear my words
Then you won't take away my hurt...You can't,
you won't take away my pain,
you won't take away my injustice
or my struggle. They are mine,
they belong to me. My gift...
Gifted to me
so that I can tell you what it feels like.

My gift to you, so you can make a change
so that you can make the difference. BE the difference

Don't walk away from here with tears
don't walk away from me
by doing nothing, you'd be like all the others
they chose to ignore me,
they never listened,
they never heard me,
they chose never to see me,
they looked the other way,
they didn't look after my feelings.
I had to and it's difficult when you're little
they just didn't care enough
so please, don't walk away

Please. Take away hope,
take away inspiration if you will,
take away the fact I didn't give up,
I didn't give in. Though I came so close.
Believe me, my 'belief' though small,
held my 'me pieces' together,
it stopped me breaking apart.

Go out there, don't make the difference,
don't just say it,
feel it, do it, **be the difference**
I ain't talking sweeping gesture,
the smallest things really are the most important,
A smile,
a touch that doesn't hurt
a small word of praise
a little word of encouragement
and sometimes that's enough
cos It means I can look up
I can think about tomorrow,
I can dream
I can get through today

and I will know you heard me

AUTHORS

About the Authors

- *Anonymous*

A care experienced social worker currently working as a supervising social worker in a fostering service. Has previous experience of working as a social worker for children and young people in a Local Authority setting on a children in care team, working on government initiated pilots and an author of research on children in care. Has always been a fierce advocate for providing young people in care with best service and genuinely wanting children in care to be given the best opportunities in life.

- Carolina Caires

Shout out - Mary Carter and Carly Banks

- David Anderson

David is a care experienced activist who pushes for the necessary changes to ensure all care experienced people, past and present, can realise their rights and full potential. He is a father and a foster carer to three children with his wife. Together, in France, they run a therapeutic farm where they welcome anyone who may benefit from the mixture of animals, nature, and connection.

David also teaches social work students and social educators with importance on love, respect and equality for people experiencing the care system. David is looking forward to working collaboratively to ensure the social work profession understands and values the experience of care as it relates to practice.

Shout out - In memory of Thomas Hutchison

Social media - @RunAskol

- *David Grimm*

David Grimm is a social work student with experience of foster care, kinship care, residential care and the impact of being under the supportive efforts of multiple social workers. He is also a poet and artist, with most of his efforts aiming towards poetry as he finds it therapeutic and diverse as a creative art form. After he qualifies David hopes to work alongside unaccompanied children and support them in either: returning to their families or setting up a new life that finds the children thriving as much as possible. He also hopes to study social work in other countries in order to better understand care experience as it stands throughout the world as opposed to the local knowledge that he currently holds. This of course all depends on David achieving his qualifications and becoming a practicing social worker but he feels very confident that with the support and love of his current friend group and colleagues, he can pass with no issues, ready and able to be a practical and wholesome support to those he works with.

Shoutout - I would like to give a special mention to Judy Furnivall, Dr. Graham Connelly, and Dr. Laura Steckley. It is and always has been my belief that I wouldn't have made it to university without the support and encouragement of these individuals (as well as many more) and a particular gratitude for bearing with me through my more stubborn and self-sabotaging years, thank you beyond words and I can't wait to continue being your friend and colleague once I'm a qualified practitioner.

I would love to give an enormous thanks to Siobhan and Mary for every effort that has gone into this book, from intention to production, this book is undoubtedly a fantastic tool that will allow social workers to better understand care experienced people...I am so grateful for champions such as yourself being in the social work world.

Finally, and absolutely not least two of the most influential women in my life: Kirsten and Nikita, who, alongside Laura, Judy and Graham encouraged my education, but also literally kept me alive and are massively impactful on my views, values and everything I am passionate about in life.

Thank you to you all.

I am and will forever be, indescribably grateful to know you and be your friend x

Social media - @Davethecarebear

- Elizabeth Tusting

I am a social worker qualified for 25 years working with children and families. I started my career working in the behaviour support service and with young people with challenging behaviour before moving into children's social care, where I was involved in implementing the Leaving Care Act before managing the team. From there I went on to manage all of the teams for 'Looked After' (children in care) services. As a former looked after child, I have a passionate interest in the provision of high quality, sustainable and reparative foster placements and about the delivery of sensitive and effective services for children in care. I am especially curious about the emotional impact of trauma and abuse upon children and young people. I graduated from the Tavistock where along with my studies I have undertaken research in this area for my MA. Specifically, I completed a thesis about "The attitude, views and emotional experience of children's allocated workers when working with disrupted foster care placements". I developed what I understand to be the first therapeutic fostering service nationally, collaborating with like-minded professionals to develop the model further and an accredited certificate in therapeutic fostering. I have consulted with other local authorities and independent fostering agencies to share and implement the model.

I am committed to supporting and developing other professionals as I know that to deliver services of the highest quality and standard requires a thoughtful, nurturing and containing management and a leadership style that cultivates a facilitating environment from which professionals can grow and learn.

Finally, my greatest achievement is that I am a very proud mum of my two sons and two grandsons.

Shoutout - I wish to acknowledge Mary Carter for her patience and persistence in encouraging me to write this piece and in doing so, providing a welcome and unexpected little adventure in my journey through life.

- Hannah Ide

I am twenty-seven years old and currently completing my ASYE year within a child protection team. I recently graduated from the University of Chichester with first class honours in social work, which is one of my greatest achievements. I live by the seaside with my partner Dean. I enjoy drinking cocktails, shopping, playing Xbox, the cinema and even going to bingo! I am very passionate about the rights of looked after children, especially with regards to mental wellbeing and criminalisation. I do not know what the future holds but for now my goal is to continue supporting vulnerable children the best I can and be the social worker I wish I'd had when I was younger!

- Ian Dickson

Born into a Scottish itinerant family, my large sibling group were split up and placed in different local authorities in different countries. We were never reunited as a family. One sibling had his name changed and was unofficially "adopted" by his foster carers. It was over 40 years before I met him for the first time. I spent 16 years in care as a child in the 1950's and 1960's. Abused for 6 years in residential care, it was the later love of a foster parent which saved my life when I was discharged from care to homelessness at 18. She believed in me, took me in and gave me a home long before "Staying Put". Against the odds and without external support, I was one of the less than 1% of care experienced people who made it to university back then, albeit in my 20's. I spent over 40 years as a social worker, manager in residential care settings and Ofsted inspector. I have campaigned for young people in care for almost half a century. I was the founder and Chair of the "Conference for Care Experienced People" in 2019. A conference for care experienced people of ALL ages, from all social settings and in all their diversity, it was the only one of its kind ever to take place. I am a happily married unremarkable father and grandfather. My ordinary life shows the negative myths about care experienced people are simply not true.

Shoutout - My thoughts go out to a tiny working-class lady with little education but a heart the size of a cathedral. "Auntie May" was more than a foster parent. She was more a mother to me and a grandmother to my daughter. For all the fine words our social work "leaders" speak from their offices daily, this little lady will always be the personification of loving social work to me.

Social Media - @IDickson258

- Ian Thomas

Ian is a qualified social worker with professional experience of working in international childcare reform, working within a foundation that supports Non-Governmental Organisations (NGO's) and Governments with an agenda towards de-institutionalisation. Ian has ten years' experience of working in the UK foster care sector offering training and support to foster carers and children and young people engagement and participation. Ian is a passionate activist / public speaker presenting his learning on the internal and external factors impacting children, young people and adults affected by alternative care, addiction and marginalisation on international platforms. Ian is on a personal mission to continue to understand self and inspire understanding and compassion towards human adversity.

Ian is a former looked after child, who lived with around 20 families and several children's homes. Ian left care aged 16 and entered into the criminal justice system shortly after, resulting in three years of life incarcerated through a battle with class A drug addiction. Over the past 12 years his recovery has been one of personal development and educational attainment.

Shoutout - The people and organisations that loved me through it all, the Forward Trust, Clear Minds International - Dwayne, Kathryn and Jacquie. My friends, who are also my family so many to mention but Yusuf, Afshan and Jan I will eternally be grateful to. Two fellow trauma survivors and inspirations Earl and Eleanor. Every human being journeying with me - thank you.

Social Media -
Twitter: @ianpresents
LinkedIn: linkedin.com/in/ian-thomas-5b573a100
Facebook: https://www.facebook.com/ian.thomas.54922

- Jo Thompson

I started my professional experience as a residential social worker before going to university as a mature student to study social work. My experience as a qualified social worker ranges from children with disabilities, to hospital social work and in recent years, adoption.

Shoutout - James, for your love and unwavering support. Millie and Archie, who taught me to be a Mum and a better social worker.

In loving memory of Saul. Who always held me in mind.

- *Karin Heber*

Karin Heber is a registered social worker/social pedagogue with over 20 years' experience. She currently works as a Professional Officer with the Scottish Association for Social Worker (SASW). Practice background pre- and post-qualifying spans work with people with mental ill-health and/or disabilities, children, young people and their families in statutory, voluntary or residential settings in Germany and Scotland. Practice educator, Family Group Decision Making (FGDM) coordinator and independent social work consultant. Climate activist.

Shoutout - Dedicated to my sister and brother, my partner Ted and my friends in case you have any doubts how cherished you are.

Social Media -

www.linkedin.com/in/karin-heber

@KarinHeber

INSIDERS OUTSIDERS

- *Kyla*

I came to the UK as a child and spent from the age of 12-18 in the public care system. Once I left care, I found employment in the social care sector, initially starting my career in the youth offending team before moving on to work with adults with learning disabilities. I then relocated after meeting my husband and worked with youth homelessness before having a career break to have my children.

Since 2012 I have worked in residential care and with young people who display harmful behaviour. In 2018 I started my degree in Social Work qualifying in 2021. I now work in long-term children's safeguarding team. I am currently studying for my master's degree in Social Pedagogical leadership and hope to contribute to service development going forward.

Shoutouts - There are so many individuals I wish to acknowledge, and I am unable to mention them all here. But here is a shout out to the individuals that have been by my side and in my heart as I started the journey into social work.

Big shout out to Youlanda you have been unwavering in your support for me over the years - you are amazing.

Kate - your insight and support was pivotal to my journey; I am unsure I would have completed my degree without those conversations - Thank you!

Sadia - your humility, humour, food, and personality got me through some tough challenges with a smile.

Jo - Your impact on me and my learning can never be overstated - thank you. You have inspired my love of learning and led me to believe that I could not only 'survive' university but could 'thrive'.

Juliette – Thank you for always being my Cheerleader- no matter how tough things got.

Tracy – you are one of my inspirations and your belief in me, encouraged me to try believing in myself - you have my heart always.

Emma and Kim – Thank you for listening, hearing, and encouraging me to develop my practice, your support has made a big difference to my transition from 'student to social worker'.

Last but by no means least! Colette, Nicki and Gemma, I am so lucky to be starting my social work journey with you by my side.

And my three children – you are the reason I get back up and try my best every day.

- *Laura Bye*

Care experienced professional trying to inspire hope, positivity and improved outcomes for all. Everything I do is based on strengths based, empowering approaches.

Shoutout - Care experienced and oppressed individuals in society who desperately need a voice and a glimpse of hope, do not let trauma be a life sentence.

Mostly importantly to Mary and Siobhan for allowing me to be part of this.

Social media -

www.linkedin.com/in/laura-bye-656939158

@LauraBye5

- *Marie*

My name is Marie and I'm delighted to be contributing towards this anthology.

I am currently the Chair of Association of Care Experienced Social Care Workers. I find a lot of comfort in the group which I'm looking forward to growing with others.

Currently, I'm a senior social worker and I have worked in both statutory and non-statutory settings. I have had the privilege of meeting so many wonderful colleagues and young people.

Care was a really difficult experience for me. I found foster care very traumatic, and it took 28 placements until I was able to settle into a kind children's home. It was in this 'too expensive' placement where I finally re-joined education, made friends and went to university. My life started there. I do wonder what would have been of me had I not been funded to live there.

In my spare time I really enjoy ultra-running. I'd love to get more women into sport as we are very much under-represented. Sport can bring much joy, friendship and achievement once you find what you enjoy!

Shoutout - My wonderful social worker Pam who stuck with me through it all. She is now a dear friend.

Social Media - Mazz4713

- *Mike. S*

I experienced care during the 80's, 90's and 00's. I entered (and exited) care 14 times over this time, between my mother's care and 8 different carers.

Since turning 18 I started working with children in schools as a learning mentor and then spend several years as a youth worker.

In 2011 I qualified as a social worker and have been a social work manager since 2018. I have worked across safeguarding teams, fostering teams, children in care and care leaver teams and reunification from care teams.

I am currently a PhD candidate looking at transitions from care and the independence – interdependence dichotomy.

Social Media - Twitter: @MikeDS2020

- *Narges Qauyumi*

Narges Qauyumi was born in Kabul, the capital city of Afghanistan. She sought asylum in the UK with her family in 2001 entering through the typical roots portrayed in mainstream media. Narges entered the care system at the age of 17 where she focused on her education knowing this was key to her success.

It took Narges three failed attempts at A-levels before realising that something needed to change. These reflections led to her embracing social work as a career path. During her 1st year of University Narges became a Connected Person Carer to her sister at the age of 20. She went on to complete a BA Honours in Psychosocial Studies at the University of East London in 2017.

Having successfully fostered her sister for 5 years Narges entered mainstream fostering where she embraced the role of being a care experienced foster carer. Narges was adamant and determined that social work was indeed her career path. It was this determination which led her to complete her MA Degree in Social Work at Nottingham Trent University. Narges qualified as a social worker in 2021 during the Covid-19 Pandemic.

Shoutout - Dedicated to my two precious goats Alyana and Qais. To my sister Dana who has pushed me to be the mother I am to my children today. Fai my foster daughter for teaching me to love in a very different way. My husband Bilal honestly just for simply being there, though he is still a lazy bum like many other husbands out there.

Finally, to Jacqueline Buntyn my personal advisor from when I was in care; Tracey Coulson my supervising social worker from Enfield Social Care, Judith Cooper, Bryony Tetlow,

Nadia Islam and Shellah Ali both in the capacity of colleagues and friends; truly amazing inspirational women I am grateful to have crossed paths with.

Social Media -

Twitter: @Narges_NQ

LinkedIn: Narges Qauyumi

- Naz

I am currently a second year master's student at University of Birmingham.

My inspiration to study social work comes from my own lived experience. I have experienced positive as well as negative interventions from social workers. However, growing up being a social worker was never the original plan it was something that I found myself in. My undergrad was in fine art, and I had exhibited a few works in London and Northampton. I set up a media business and built myself up in terms of my creative development. Whilst setting up a business I actively volunteered within the community and worked alongside Change Grow Live to support young care leavers develop their confidence and provide support for them to engage in education, training, or employment. I established a relationship with Birmingham Children's Trust and other professional agencies to aid young care leavers. It was through this employment I felt inspired to become a social worker.

Shout out -

To my family and friends

Joanne Smith (Personal Advisor for care leavers at Birmingham Children's Trust)

- *Rebecca Olayinka*

Rebecca Olayinka is a qualified social worker, freelance writer and speaker who lives in London UK.

Rebecca was born in Hackney, London UK, however she lived in foster care for the first 9.5 years of her life in Clacton-on-Sea (Essex) with her foster mother and after moved back to Hackney with her birth mother.

Rebecca has always had a love of writing and has been writing since she was 13 mainly poetry and some short stories.

Rebecca spent many years studying and working in Bristol where she attended UWE Bristol and completed her social work degree. Rebecca worked has worked in adult care throughout her 10 year career, where she has worked at senior practitioner level; her specialisms are Adult Safeguarding, Preparing for Adulthood (transitions) and Best Interest Assessments.

Rebecca has also completed a HR CIPD course and is an Associate Member of the CIPD. Rebecca has also served on the core leadership team in Bristol City Council's (BCC) staff lead Black Minority and Ethnic Employees Group (BMEEG) from 2018-2019.

Rebecca has further been developing her leadership skills by volunteering on the core committee for the Black Minority Ethnic Group in BCC to support leading the wider group from 2020-2021.

Rebecca is very passionate about Black Foster Children as she was a care experienced child and aims to change the experience for Black foster children within the UK.

Rebecca is also an independent member of a fostering panel for a local authority in London where she lives.

Rebecca has had her written work featured in 2 books:

Outlanders - Hidden Narratives from Social Workers of Colour and Chicken Soup For The Soul - I'm Speaking Now: Black Women Share Their Truth in 101 Stories of Love, Courage and Hope.

Rebecca has written various articles and poetry pieces for the online magazine The Everyday Magazine who have really encouraged and supported her creative expression. Rebecca has also had some speaking opportunities; such as being a guest on a YouTube Channel by a feminist focused interviewer on the topic of Black Foster Children in Care. Rebecca has been on Ujima (a Bristol based radio station) Rebecca has also appeared as a guest on podcasts. In addition, Rebecca also loves dancing and baking as other ways of honing her creative expression.

Shoutout - Marceline A. M. Vroome (1919-1993)

Grace A. Olayinka (1945-2008)

Social Media -
Facebook: www.facebook.com/RebeccaOlayinka
Instagram: Rebeccaloves2laugh
Twitter: @RebeOlayinka
LinkedIn: Rebecca Olayinka

- *Rebekah Pierre*

Rebekah Pierre is a care experienced social worker, author, and professional officer at the British Association of Social Workers. Combining a passion for social work and arts-based practice, her book, 'Gymtherapy: Developing emotional well-being and resilience in children through the medium of movement' explores how to bring direct work to life through choreography and embodiment. Having supported children and families in various contexts in Chile, Spain and the UK, she brings an international perspective to her work. She is also a freelance journalist who writes about gender, social care and class.

Shoutout - I would like to thank my late nana, from whom I developed a love for words. She worked 3 jobs to give me opportunities she never had – to pay for music, dance and drama lessons where I learnt to express myself with my whole heart. I think of her whenever I am given an opportunity to do so.

Social Media - @Rebekahpierre92
uk.linkedin.com/in/rebekah-pierre-223b04122

ABOUT THE AUTHORS

- *Richard Devine*

Richard Devine is a Consultant social worker for Bath and North East Somerset Council. He has worked with children and families since he qualified in 2010. He has a Masters in Attachment Studies and is trained in several attachment procedures. His vision is a child protection system that does not involve the necessity to permanently remove children from their families.

Social Media -
Blog: richarddevinesocialwork.com/
Twitter: twitter.com/richarddevinesw

- *Saira-Jayne Jones*

Saira-Jayne Jones is an artist, poet, social worker and lived experience practitioner based in the West Midlands.

Her pieces are often a reflection of her experience, taking you on a journey through a range of themes including identity, mental health, trauma, abuse and adversity. The pieces Saira-Jayne creates can be as intriguing as they are challenging, honest and raw; heavily influenced by aspects of her identity as a female, disabled, lesbian, care experienced adult who wrangles with the complexities of trauma and mental health. Her colourful yet chaotic approach to her artworks style, she brands as 'complex post chaotic creativity', which is informed by her upbringing in what she affectionately terms a 'comfortably curious place called Chelmsley Wood', seasoned with the struggles of growing up in poverty on the margins of society.

Through her art Saira-Jayne endeavours to bring to the forefront all that we often shy away from in society, approaching difficult and taboo subjects, providing insight through experience, challenging inequality, and injustice, and reflecting upon the impact of a life defined by the views, labels, judgements, misconceptions, and stigma that exist within the fabric of our language, values and culture.

Saira-Jayne's rationale for creating is as varied as the pieces which she creates, with her poetry and artworks reflecting a juxtapose of confrontation vs. escapism. One thing that is very clear from the pieces she creates is that they evolve from a place of feeling. Her pieces take you on a journey which navigates both internal and external worlds, examining uncomfortable truths, confronting preconceived ideas, enabling self-expression, and facilitating a conversation with her audience. As an exhibiting artist she enjoys the opportunity to discuss the thought-provoking nature of her work and hear the perspectives of others. In terms of visual art Saira-Jayne acknowledges that the pieces she creates enable her to speak without speaking, facilitating a deeper level of connection when her imagery is shared alongside her words.

'As humans we are hard wired for connection. I not only discovered a deeper connection with myself through creativity and art, but also that I could connect with others through this medium too.'

Saira-Jayne's art and creativity are not only a vehicle for self-exploration and discovery but are also a useful tool in working with others to discover, unlock, explore, and celebrate their own creativity. Saira-Jayne is co-founder of the organisation Artifacts www.artifactscep.org.uk where she uses art, poetry and creative approaches combined with lived experience to engage with people in a range of settings; delivering creative based workshops, bespoke training packages, art and verse led discussions, consultancy and exhibitions. In her role Saira-Jayne draws upon her varied range of lived experience and creative approaches to also engage with care experienced individuals of all ages, and to provide insight and understanding to those organisations, professionals and significant adults who work with and around care experienced people.

Shoutout - To my soul sibling Yusuf Paul McCormack, my sister Emma, my wife Caz, Amanda Knowles and Maria Francis for believing in me even when I do not believe in myself.

Social media -
Twitter: @poisonpinkdaisy / @Artifac22171753
Instagram: @ArtbySaira-JayneJones
Linkin: @Saira-Jayne Jones

- *Dr Trevor Rodgers-Gray*

I am a parent. I am a social worker. I am a care leaver.

My care heritage includes a residential children's home and foster care. I gained my master's degree in social work in 2007 from the University of York and have been in practice or social work education ever since.

I am registered with Social Work England, and am a proud member of BASW, the Care Leavers Association, and the Association of Care Experienced Social Care Workers.

My practice experience was largely working alongside children and young people. I worked at Barnardo's as a social worker and then a Children's Service Manager. Before this I worked for a local authority supporting adults with a learning disability.

I held a temporary social work lecturer post at the University of Plymouth, and after this gained a permanent lectureship at Bradford College (since April 2012) where I subsequently became programme lead for the Social Work BA, and then Head of School for Social Care and Community Practice (from September 2019). As the Head of School, I designed and gained validation and approval for the social work degree apprenticeship programme.

I joined the University of Bradford in January 2021 as a social work lecturer / assistant professor and became the programme lead for the MA Social Work degree in October 2021. I am open about my care experience at the university and am supported by both colleagues and the institution. My care heritage is central to my teaching and research, and who I am, my identity. Care experience is a recognised identity within the university's Equality, Diversity, and Inclusion Committee, of which I am a member.

My research, academic and practice interests are diverse, and include the following:

- care-experienced social workers / social work students.

- the experiences of care leavers (notions of 'home', class, belonging and inclusion).

- the efficacy and foundations of the pro-feminist movement: The White Ribbon Campaign.

Along with colleagues at the University of Bradford I have developed international links with the Arctic University of Norway and Bielefeld University, Germany, and am an ambassador for The White Ribbon Campaign. I look at care from both sides now.

Shoutout - I wish to acknowledge my colleagues at the University of Bradford for their support, in particular, Brian Mitchell, Robert Strachan, Paul Sullivan, Clare Beckett-Wrighton, and Hannah Intezar. Also, Jim Goddard, chair of the CLA, and my friends within the ACESCWs, David Grimm and Ian Dickson, amongst others. Finally, my deep love for my children, Liam, and Eva, with whom I belong.

Social media - Twitter: @TrevorRodgersGr

- *Victoria J*

Social worker and manager of a fostering team in the North West.

Merseyside Born and bred.

Mum of two and Novice Double Bass player.

Pandemic podcaster for student learning.

Shoutout - Dr Jadweiga Leigh

Childhood friend Keely O'Keefe

The late Mrs Hope, Mrs Ellis and the Brooks family

Social media - @victoriajenks

- *Victoria-Maria*

I left foster care aged 16 and fell pregnant two months later. Aware of the challenges ahead, I was keen to build my path in life. I drew from the strength I had developed throughout my childhood experiences in children's homes and foster placements. Reflecting on my difficult start in life, I decided to pursue a career in social work, and I am currently studying for a BA (Hons) in Social Work at the University of Essex. My ambition is to dismantle harmful systems and challenge discriminative cultures that alienate care experienced students from their communities. I genuinely appreciate the challenges for care leavers entering further education, and I am the founder of 'Talking Back'. A platform for care experienced students to share and discuss ways education providers can support and facilitate their time in education, guided by the principles of inclusion.

Shoutout - Thank you, Jared, for *listening* to my voice when many had only heard it.